The Healthcare Collapse

Where We've Been and
Where We Need to Go

The Healthcare Collapse

Where We've Been and
Where We Need to Go

Eldo E. Frezza, MD, MBA, FACS

Routledge
Taylor & Francis Group

A PRODUCTIVITY PRESS BOOK

A Routledge title, part of the Taylor & Francis imprint, a member of the Taylor & Francis Group, the academic division of T&F Informa plc

Published in 2019 by Routledge
Taylor & Francis Group
711 3rd Avenue
New York, NY 10017

International Standard Book Number-13: 978-1-138-58110-4 (Hardback)

Library of Congress Cataloging-in-Publication Data

Names: Frezza, Eldo E., author.
Title: The healthcare collapse : where we've been and where we need to go / Eldo Frezza.
Description: Boca Raton : Taylor & Francis, 2019. | Includes bibliographical references and index.
Identifiers: LCCN 2018020486 (print) | LCCN 2018022125 (ebook) | ISBN 9780429506925 (e-Book) | ISBN 9781138581104 (hardback : alk. paper)
Subjects: | MESH: Health Services Administration | Delivery of Health Care | Managed Care Programs | Physician's Role | United States
Classification: LCC RA412.3 (ebook) | LCC RA412.3 (print) | NLM W 84 AA1 | DDC 368.38/2--dc23
LC record available at https://lccn.loc.gov/2018020486

Visit the Taylor & Francis Web site at
http://www.taylorandfrancis.com

and the CRC Press Web site at
http://www.crcpress.com

This book is for all the physicians that are striving for high quality in the face of the difficult healthcare environment, the ones that struggle, the ones who are depressed or affected by moral injury.

It is for all the physicians who wrote their frustration about healthcare collapsing and from whom I took inspiration for this book.

For all the corporations and hospitals that are supporting the physicians and care about their physical and mental wellness.

For my two sons: Edoardo and Gianmarco who always pushed me to do more and better.

Contents

SECTION II PHYSICIAN STRUGGLES

SECTION III BROKEN SYSTEM

Synopsis

The evolution of the healthcare system in the U.S. has seen numerous changes in the last 30 years where fee-for-service was the mainstay of reimbursement models, hospitals were managed by physicians, and patient care was key. The early 1990s saw the emergence of HMOs and other managed care models with physicians handing over leadership roles to corporate entities whose main concern was the bottom line and profitability, and patient care and satisfaction suffered.

While managed care reimbursement models have improved and are more patient-centric, the vast majority of hospitals and health systems are still run by business people with very little knowledge of medicine and what is truly involved in caring for the patient. We evaluated the Medicare crises and the Medicaid funding, and this book also challenges the idea of a single payer and the never-ending healthcare reform. Incentive programs such as ACOs and pay for performance are not improving patient care and have been failing.

This book looks at where healthcare has been, with the deep crises among and toward the physicians, who are excluded from the decision-making arenas. The book recommends solutions to create a system that focuses on the patient and providing quality care in this age of reimbursement cuts, demands for better technology and providing a safer environment for both the patient and clinicians who work in hospitals. The author also advocates for a shift in management and recommends hospital leaders engage more physicians in process improvement and other initiatives which can result in a more efficient system – one where quality patient care dominant. The book also outlines patient engagement activities, community health outreach and education programs.

Key Points

- Describes the evolution of healthcare from what it was to what it is now.
- Discusses how health systems have gone from physician-led entities, to systems managed by business people with no experience in medicine or how to care for patients.

- Takes a look at Medicare and Medicaid, its evolution and what the future holds for these entitlement programs.
- Suggests how healthcare could and should look in the future with more patient engagement and more physician involvement in the management of hospitals and health systems and why.

Author

 **Eldo E. Frezza** was born and raised in Venice, attended medical school in Italy, and completed his postgraduate training as a resident in the United States. He has also obtained a Masters in Business Administration from Texas Tech University. He is a Fellow of the American College of Surgeons (FACS), American Medical Association, and American Medical Physician Leadership.

Dr. Frezza is an award-winning physician executive who elevates organizational performance and aligns physicians to the rapidly changing healthcare landscape. He embraces and skillfully navigates the challenges of complex enterprises, including rural hospitals, academic medical centers, and physician practices. His clinical background as a surgeon informs his ability to thrive in high-pressure environments, assess complex business situations, and perform thoughtful analysis to identify affordable, sustainable solutions.

CEO and founder of Cure Your Practice (www.cureyourpractice.com), Dr. Frezza has over 20 years of experience in providing consulting services to healthcare organizations in the areas of metrics, supply chains, clinical service line development, organizational strategy, alignment, and network formation. This includes healthcare systems, academic medical centers, physician groups, insurance companies, and government agencies, as well as professional organizations.

As a medical director of quality and vice president of medical affairs, he has guided the boardroom decision-making that has defined the priorities and direction of many leading healthcare organizations to ensure high quality and ethical value.

Dr. Frezza is the author of three essential textbooks on ethics, business, and laparoscopic surgery and has written numerous articles on clinical practice, research, economics, and ethics. He is also the author of several books on sociology and fiction. Dr. Frezza has written eight books with well-known publishers and has published more than 200 articles in peer-reviewed journals and book chapters. His bestselling book is a diet book, which continues to sell ten years after the second edition was published.

Dr. Frezza has written books for his college classes and tested them on his students. He has always worked on motivation and how to make society better by teaching, demonstrating, and explaining the basic principles of societal ethics, civic responsibility, and wellness. These opportunities have helped students find a better pathway in life. Dr. Frezza makes his books easy to read, to which his students attest that the attraction of his writing is that the book can be read in a single sitting.

He has been a full professor and professor of ethics in several institutions, among them Texas A&M, Texas Tech, and University of Pittsburgh. He has won several writing contests, is a regular speaker on ethics, sociology, and medicine for various medical societies, and is the editor of several medical journals.

Dr. Frezza started out as a journalist before attending medical school. He speaks three languages; he has often been considered a Renaissance man since his background goes beyond medical specialties and into ethics, business, sociology, and philosophy.

He has also served as a commander of the Texas Medical Rangers for West Texas.

Introduction: Review Our Mistakes and Look to the Future

The fact that the healthcare system is in crisis seems not to be news to anybody. It is a crisis cycle that will repeat itself until we can fix or reform the system.

United States (US) healthcare was almost nonexistent at the beginning of the last century and through the Kaiser Company, which paid insurance to attract workers to build ships, health maintenance organizations (HMOs) and now the Affordable Care Act (ACO) became a reality.

The federal government was instrumental in the 1960s in setting up Medicare and Medicaid, but that was not enough. Healthcare was given to the private sector, and mostly for profit.

This was both good and bad. Undoubtedly, the level of care in the US has reached the highest point globally and is well-recognized. Unfortunately, everything is private, and costs have been skyrocketing beyond the need and average costs in other countries.

It should be impossible that the US has the highest healthcare costs, despite high levels of achievement and excellent care. If you look at Sweden or Norway, their healthcare works quite well – hospitals provide excellent healthcare. Germany is another example where healthcare is of the highest quality. Not to go too far, Canada delivers excellent healthcare, and some Canadian doctors have also been practicing in the US.

The US spent $8,233 on health per person in 2010. Norway, the Netherlands, and Switzerland are the next highest spenders, but in the same year, they each spent at least $3,000 less per person than the US. The average spending on healthcare among the 33 other developed countries was $3,268 per person.

So, wondering what happened to US healthcare is not a question anymore, since no answer has been found for years. The question is how we can fix it.

It's like a never-ending story that will never end until a crash occurs. This book will show that Medicare and Medicaid are destined to crash in 2025 based on a statistical model. How can we adjust this?

If we want to fix this problem, we need everybody involved to disregard their own interests and for once think exclusively about the public's interest and the interests of the patient as a duty to their country.

Healthcare is a right to which every patient it is entitled, as has been outlined by the United Nations and the World Health Organization. Healthcare is supposed to be given indiscriminately to everybody because this is what is supposed to be right for everybody.

It should not be considered socialism or communism, but simply a human civil right.

Bernie Sanders wrote: "Health care must be recognized as a right, not a privilege. Every man, woman, and child in our country should be able to access the health care they need regardless of their income. We need a system that works for all of us. We need a system that prioritizes the health of all working-class families over the profits of insurance companies."[1]

On the opposite side, if healthcare is not regulated, costs will skyrocket. Physicians will not accept government payments because they have decreased tremendously and physicians have a family and kids to send to college, too. It is outrageous that a surgeon gets paid $50 to take out an appendix, for example.

"Treating medical care as a commodity means temporary shortages, and it means that some people will not get everything we would wish them to have. But that's also true of government-sponsored medical care, as the most honest advocates will admit. And whereas government-sponsored medical care requires a top-down approach that violates individual liberties, generates overdemand, and quashes supply, markets prize individual liberties, reduce demand (you demand less of what you must pay for), and heighten supply through profit incentive."[2]

We need to eliminate insurance silos whereby a plan bought in Kentucky does not work in Texas and vice versa, meaning that there is no freedom in healthcare in the US as there is in other countries. In Italy, for example, if you have healthcare, you can be treated in Sicily or Milan without extra or higher copayments or increased out-of-pocket expenses.

Mystification of the healthcare costs paid to the doctor should finally be taken out of the equation. The cost of healthcare is not the cost of the doctor but the cost of the hospital and the insurance. The doctors receive 10%–20% of patients' bills. Where, then, do all of these enormous expenses go? That's what everybody wants to know.

Accusing doctors of making too much money, as some financial leaders have claimed, does not solve the problem. The suggestion to bring more foreign graduates to the US will not address the problem; every medical school in the US would close because, in other countries, medical school costs less than $10,000 while in the US you end up with a $500,000 loan to pay back after your schooling.

Most of the administrators in charge of healthcare come from manufacturing industries and don't have a grasp on healthcare. Business knowledge is essential, but without an understanding of what the healthcare industry requires, it is difficult to be successful. It is like fighting in a war as a general without ever having been a soldier first. You will never understand what the soldier has to go through.

This is the time to restructure the healthcare system from the position where more physicians are needed to function as administrators. It is time to stop thinking about margins and political benefit and work for the benefit of the population.

We need to learn from our past mistakes to reform healthcare with an excellent plan for improving healthcare that is not based on politics or influenced by Washington.

We need to level costs and charges without ballooning them to benefit a few. Decreased costs of medication or the ability to buy medications from other countries should be allowed. This will decrease the influence of Big Pharma on healthcare reform. We need clear and open communication that is not limited by politics and personal interests.

A classic example of our failure to learn from history is the Afghanistan war. For the past 4,000 years, many different influential cultures and nations have been trying to conquer Afghanistan. From the Egyptian to the Persian Empires, from the Roman to the Byzantine Empires, from Germany during the Second World War to the Russians, all have failed. The US thought they were better, but they achieved a similar result. That should make people think.

Ethics is also an important influence that needs to be applied to healthcare. The ethical goals in healthcare are to take care of people, and not of the business. The business will succeed if the ethical principles are there.

We need a society that works for all, which is not to be confused with communism but with "stoicism." Civic duty is nothing but social ethics or the unspoken norms of society. It is not just about keeping the roads, streets, and public property clean, but also has to do with abiding by the law, respecting others' point of view, and respecting places and towns and each other.

Was Marx's idea of society the most socialized and equal for all? Probably not, after seeing how this idea has been wrongly applied to certain Eastern countries. Did Nietzsche, the German philosopher, have a better idea for society? His writings on truth, morality, language, aesthetics, cultural theory, history, nihilism, power, consciousness, and the meaning of existence have exerted an enormous influence on Western philosophy and the intellectual past, but have also taken a turn in the direction of nationalism and Nazism.[3]

We need a society that will work for everybody, and we have to work together to achieve the same goals and leave our own interests permanently to one side to achieve the perfect system.

Healthcare is composed of health, policies, strategy, etc. and care for the patient to achieve better health for him or her. This last task only the physician can perform.

We need to place physicians at the center of healthcare once again, by having:

1. Physicians working in administration
2. Administrators that are specialized in healthcare and can really understand what it means to work at a hospital
3. The physician's job and quality priced fairly, disregarding cheap rumors and perceptions.

Notes

1. Bernie Sanders. Medicare for All. Available at: https://berniesanders.com/medicareforall/.
2. Ben Shapiro. 2017, January 11. Health Care Is a Commodity, Not a Right. *National Review*. Available at: https://www.nationalreview.com/2017/01/health-care-markets-government-commodity-human-right/.
3. Angel J. Candelairo Rodriguez. 2013, March 19. About Author's Ambition. Available at: https://angelcandelario1.wordpress.com/category/technical-writing-quotes/page/2/.

Suggested Reading

1. Should All Americans Have the Right (Be Entitled) To Healthcare – https://health-care.procon.org/view.answers.php?questionID=001602.
2. Health Care Industry: Markets Work Better than Government – http://www.nationalreview.com/article/443737/health-care-industry-markets-work-b.

THE EVOLUTION OF HEALTHCARE

Chapter 1

From HMO to ACA to Value: Transforming Healthcare

Transforming healthcare and healthcare organizations has been ongoing since the 1960s. Challenges in enforcing the Affordable Care Act (ACA), the CHIP program, the initiative for Medicaid-Medicare taxes, and the creation of the Accountability Care Organization (ACO), and now the repealing of the ACA, have kept legislators and the public very busy. Still, we do not see an end to this. The lack of funding on a federal level, the shifting of costs to the state to support Medicaid, and the increased premiums that those without health insurance face because of the sky-rocketing cost of healthcare has been a daily nightmare for millions of Americans.

Further transformation is on the edge of these changes, and the way that we respond to these changes will define our healthcare and society in the future.

Healthcare Evolution

Reimbursement

First Insurance

The first healthcare insurance in the United States was established by Justin Kimbal under the board of trustees of the University of Texas, in creating the Blue Cross in 1930.

Stage 1

Cost Reimbursement

This is based on the following factors:

- most hospitals were nonprofit corporations
- run by a charitable organization
- the payment method chosen was cost reimbursement

In cost reimbursement, payment is made according to the length of hospital stay; therefore, more extended hospital stays increase hospital reimbursement. Insurance companies pass the additional cost to the employer, and the insurance companies increase the premiums. Rarely do they question the validity of the provider charges. The employer is more than happy to leave the patient in the hospital for longer. Eventually the patient will have to pay the bill through higher premiums.

Stage 2

First HMO

In an effort to recruit workers for building ships during the Second World War, Kaiser offered employee health benefits in 1940. To recruit employees without violating wage controls, he began offering his employees health benefits. His program used a prospective payment system called capitation. Under the capitation payment system, the healthcare provider receives a fixed amount per patient, per month to provide specific services, often for consultation of patient and outpatient services offered. The doctor gets this manual, regardless of whether the patient needs medical assistance or not. Therefore, the system provides an incentive to keep the patient well. If the patient becomes ill, the physician is encouraged to use the most cost-effective resources to heal him or her. Capitation payment does not provide an incentive for the physician to overutilize products and services.

A health maintenance organization (HMO) was a prospective payment or capitation. The medical society initially tried to ban HMOs, and many physicians did not participate.

What is to prevent the physician from providing the cure or the service? This is another issue that needs to be understood. The length of hospital stay is significant, given that the physician can lose money if the patient's stay is too extended. Physicians and hospitals might receive HMO bonuses at the end of the year based on how much physicians save in hospitalization.

With viable management wanting to prevent losses, under the capitation payment physicians must help with the type of medicine provided by the primary physician at the hospital, the number of cancer cases treated on an inpatient and outpatient basis, the average time to detect treatable diseases, the average length of hospital stay, mortality rates, etc.

Stage 3

No HMO Restrictions

In 1980, federal legislation abolished physicians' restrictions to accept HMO, and HMO became widespread across the country.

What types of payments are there today? One kind of debt is the prospective payment system. The diagnostic-related group (DRG) is a form of prospective payment under capitation, whereby the hospital receives a fixed fee per hour, per month, regardless of the service rendered.

Under capitation, there is a need to:

■ Avoid unnecessary hospital admission, decrease length of stay, and encourage prevention
■ Keep a comprehensive medical record
■ Starting bonus for a physician based on some days that the physician keeps the patient in the hospital to maintain the cost plans
■ Increase in the patient paying out-of-pocket

Stage 4

A new development is that many hospitals have now been incorporated into a corporation comprising hundreds of hospitals.

Therefore:

■ Most administrative positions have been cut.
■ A lot of things have been centrally located.
■ Many jobs have been cut in the name of healthcare cost margins.
■ The power of HMOs has been increasing, and physicians have been losing that power.
■ Hospitals face the same problem that physicians faced years ago, because the HMO is dictating the care.

Stage 5

ACA legislation passed in 2010:

■ Increased access to care – Medicaid expansion, the insurance mandate
■ Improved quality of care – fee-for-service versus value-based purchasing

- Reduced healthcare costs
- Increased population health
- Coordinated care through healthcare delivery systems

Stage 6

Access to medical care based on:

- Improved quality of care – value-based purchasing
- Reduced healthcare costs
- Coordinated care through healthcare delivery systems

Quality Crisis in Medicine: The Change in Thinking

How does a hospital make money? By ensuring a reasonable contract with HMOs, based on localization and an emphasis on prevention. The capitation payment system has been used to prevent physicians from providing unnecessary care. HMOs, with pre-certification, control the utilization of care. They tell the physician how to take care of the patient. Therefore, HMOs are trying to control the quality of care. How can we support the physician's decision? HMO control is creating a state of panic. Instead of achieving better quality of care, HMOs are pushing physicians to see more patients to increase their revenues, since the payment for single patients is now "miserable." Hospitals have the same problem; therefore, employees are being laid off. Nurses are now in charge of the care of 12 patients, instead of 6 to 8 patients. If this system is not adjusted, healthcare will become a low-quality system. We understand the concept of cost containment, but cutting costs will make everyone work more efficiently. More patients will be seen per hour. Is this what we want when we retire and need healthcare? Many students enrolling in medical school believe that medicine is too much work and that the hours are too long when a mid- to low-level manager's salary is comparable to theirs, even after only four years of college.

The Future? Transforming Healthcare

Change is unpredictable, but the healthcare organization, like any other business organization, responds to cultural change. The problem with healthcare organizations is that there are multiple stakeholders managing various sectors of the hospital, and they all have the professional ability to understand and agree or disagree on processes.

Stage 7

Value and Not Volume for the Future

The first thing that needs to be considered is that healthcare organizations must have quality and patient care in mind at all times. Next, we need to provide stakeholders with the reasons for the change to come. They then must make people and leaders understand what models they are going to have to work with, and what types of physical and emotional changes they need to achieve.

After that is in place, the organization can enforce the process in the system by keeping control of the process and system and making sure that everybody is on board with the cultural change.

Of course, continuing to improve the skill contains the change and ability to change further if needed.

Sometimes the changes are not agreeable to the stakeholders. It is essential that when the strategies are in place, there is a structure with which to apply the policy and the process.

Of utmost importance is the respect of the people and the stakeholders involved, not just in healthcare but in any business organization. An efficient communication strategy is dependent on the ability to understand the strategy and the process and on listening to the stakeholders to make further changes, which is essential in healthcare.

A strategy can be established at the level of the corporate office, but keep in mind that the same approach can work in one state and not in another. Now that corporations own different hospitals in different states, they tend to apply a similar strategy. Even within the same state, a strategy might not work. A plan might work in West Texas but will never work in South Texas or East Texas or central Texas. Corporations need to be aware of this and cater to the culture and local traditions.

Applying the same strategy will reduce variation in the process because it will improve efficiency, both clinical and administrative. But buying into the culture of the change is a crucial first step. Leadership needs to be involved in organizational and cultural change, that needs to start first.

We need to have a value and measure of value, which usually represents safety and quality rather than financial metrics.

Most of the time, I'm a witness of the main office organization people coming down telling what they want to do and if the physician agrees. Well, if the physician doesn't agree tough for them. People are not ready to listen and are not prepared to apply changes that can be beneficial to the application of the success.

Nowadays, with electronic medical records, the transformation needs to be based on technology to integrate patient data and access to continuous care. There is no room for fragmented care; individuals from different specialties can access the data. The goal is to realize that quality needs attention across specialties.

Care, therefore, should be organized around the patient and not around the provider. Accountability by all of the care team, and not just a single physician, is required. This is because we can use electronic medical records and therefore create what we call *longitudinal continuous healthcare* that is grounded in evidence-based medicine, avoiding silos of care from a different area of the hospital or clinics in various cities.

This approach will create value. This is important because we are aiming toward a fee for the benefit and not a cost for volume.

Unfortunately, most physicians that work for the hospital corporation are hired with bonuses based on relative value units (RVUs) base, and not by value. This may be a long-term disaster!

Suggested Reading

1. Richard E. McDermot and Kevin D. Stocks. *Code Blue*. Syracuse, UT: Traemus, 2005.
2. Eldo Frezza. The six stages of the healthcare economy: Is socialized medicine at the door? A historical review. *Journal of Social Sciences* 1(4): 197–198, 2005.
3. Eldo Frezza. Survival in the current healthcare environment: How close are we to socialized medicine? *Journal of Social Sciences* 1(4): 246–247, 2005.

Chapter 2

Accountability Care Organization and Clinical Integration

What is an Accountability Care Organization?

The Center for Medicare and Medicaid Services (CMS) required hospitals and organizations to participate in the shared saving program, beginning in 2002.

This process initiated the Accountability Care Organization (ACO). The goal of this change was to improve quality and reduce costs, and it was founded on the value-based payment system, with information technology and results being well-supported.

The reason for the changes correlated with the following findings:

- Despite spending more on healthcare, Americans had poor health outcomes, including shorter life expectancy and higher prevalence of chronic conditions.
- Affordable Care Act legislation was passed in 2010 to
  - Increase access to care – Medicaid expansion, the insurance mandate
  - Improve quality of care – fee-for-service versus value-based purchasing
  - Reduce healthcare costs

The healthcare problems have been and will be an issue for quite some time. The forecast is not that positive, and Medicare and Medicaid are having financial difficulty in sustaining their programs. The population issues include:

- 16.4 million previously uninsured individuals have gained insurance
- The uninsured rate in 2014 was 15.3%, down from 20.2% in 2013
- Medicaid has been expanded to those not previously eligible
- Preventive services are covered with no out-of-pocket expense
- A crack-down on fraud and abuse
- Significant consolidation of hospitals and insurance companies
- Increases in insurance premiums, out-of-pocket costs, and catastrophic policies

Therefore, if we look into the future, we need more focus on

1. Population health
2. Coordinated care through healthcare delivery systems

Clinical Integration

Clinical integration is centered on fostering collaboration among independent doctors and hospitals in a way that increases both the quality and efficiency of patient care. This method helps to coordinate patient care from different specialties and departments in the hospital, and is a joint venture involving the physician and/or hiring him or her under the same company with the goal of having a standard way of approaching the patient.

Clinical integration was not created to change the pattern of the physician's clinical judgment, but instead to incorporate a similar approach from a different physician.

To establish clinical integration, we need to have mechanisms in place to monitor and control healthcare services with a network of physicians who can participate and define objectives based on standard medicine, which will require the organization to be more focused on how to invest in infrastructure.

The goal is to enhance the utilization of care outcomes by fostering a culture of quality based on information technology in the way that objective data has to be excellent.

ACO Financial Risk

In general, an ACO is a legally structured arrangement between primary hospital care and specialty physicians and other providers, including rehabilitation care facilities and home healthcare, to coordinate and deliver efficient care.

The Medicare sharing safety program focused on the current fee-for-service environment; the target is therefore to have similar care among different providers. There is a responsibility for gain and loss within the organization, but not on the physician. The ACO assumes financial accountability, but this does not mean that the financial risk is not based on the participant.

The success, therefore, is based on how care is delivered and coordinated by addressing the quality of health outcomes. ACO is a non-risk-based sharing saving since it will cover some of the loss.

Quality and Cost

Independent of what is going to happen with new healthcare plans and legislation, this new value-driven business is going to be the base for future healthcare delivery since it increases quality and decreases costs based on close collaboration between hospitals and physicians.

The physician is the critical part of the ACO, and that is why clinical integration is required for its success. There is no way to improve quality and reduce costs without collaboration and integration between hospital and physician.

According to the CMS, the goal is to achieve the triple aim of

1. Better care for individuals
2. Better health for the population
3. Decreased pro capita cost of care without harm to the patient

Organizational infrastructure is also needed to check the quality of cost and outcome research for the patient and to provide educational support for physicians, patients, and healthcare practitioners.

The ability to manage financial risk and to distribute payments and savings is essential. Therefore, the system must have good payer-contracting expertise with economic and capital planning and good-quality reporting to ensure high quality and the avoidance of penalties from the CMS.

The program is still within the current fee-for-service payment environment, but soon will include the Merit-Based Incentive Payment System (MIPS) and the Medicare Access and CHIP Reauthorization Act of 2015 (MACRA) (see Chapter 25). Therefore, expertise needs to be in place to avoid penalties and problems in case the healthcare system changes. Starting with a good contract negotiation fee target and incentive payment is the initial base for proper and fruitful clinical integration.

ACO and Physicians

Most of the ACO now realizes the importance of having physicians on board.

The physician must play a vital role because he or she is critical to achieving and sustaining high quality and reducing costs.

The physician is the most important factor for clinical integration to build the delivery network needed to understand which structure is going to be in place, how it can function, and how many people are needed to put it all together with a high-level implementation plan, and to determine their schedule.

The physician needs to be free to express concerns and raise issues without being punished by the system, especially if the hospital hires them.

The physician makes the decision that drives the dollars about 80–90% of the time. Therefore, the success of ACO is directly correlated with its relationship with the physician. The structures needed for a successful ACO include an executive and a physician leadership culture of teamwork, and a strong association between physician providers and with the administrator. Free speech needs to be preserved.

Electronic medical records are a must for coordinating different hospital offices, etc.

An organized physicians' group can look for an opportunity for a new line of services, expand the range of care, etc. It can even assess the needs of the population, based on the geographical area.

If a line of service is available, the group can suggest changes or upgrades to the infrastructure, including to clinics, dialysis centers, cancer centers, ambulatory surgery centers, etc., based on real need and the availability of physicians' competencies.

If the physician is independent, he or she needs to create a physician organization (PO) that can contract with the different hospitals. Single physicians and small private practices will disappear very soon, unfortunately. The only way for an independent physician to survive is to join forces with other physicians.

It's essential that barriers among physicians are taken down, so that physicians are not pitted against each other.

The ACO should not build barriers among physicians that would make them compete and fight with each other. This is, unfortunately, current practice, but the ACO needs to understand that only by having cooperative physicians will it be successful. A clear plan for physician payment, contracting, and explanation of bonuses is required.

This will facilitate physician alignment and allow the creation of excellent clinical integration.

Clinical research in different areas that have the potential for improvement need to be discussed with the physician. This can be achieved by assessing the current market and services, strategizing priorities, and updating utilization and the financial forecast.

Suggested Reading

1. James J. Pizzo and Mark E. Grube. Kaufman, Hall & Associates, Inc. Kaufmanhall.com.
2. Thomas J. Babbo, John P. Marren and Patrick E. Deady. Clinical Integration: A Physician and Hospital Strategy for Better Quality, Enhanced Competition, and

Collective Contracting. Available at: http://www.covenanthealth.org/ForHealth Professionals/CME/CIWhitePaper-v2.pdf.

3. Stephen M. Shortell. *Remaking Health Care in America: Building Organized Delivery Systems*, First Edition. San Francisco, CA: Jossey-Bass Publishers, 1996.

4. Federal Trade Commission and the U.S. Department of Justice: Statements of Antitrust Enforcement Policy in Health Care. Available at: www.ftc.gov/bc/health-care/industryguide/policy/statement8.htm.

5. American Hospital Association. Accountable Care Organizations: AHA Research Synthesis Report. June 2010. Available at: www.aha.org/aha/content/2010/pdf/09-26-2010-Res-Synth-Rep.pdf.

6. Robert Berenson and Stephen Zuckerman. How Will Hospitals Be Affected by Health Care Reform? Robert Wood Johnson Foundation and the Urban Institute. Available at: www.urban.org/uploadedpdf/412155-Hospitals-Affected-by-Reform.pdf.

7. Don M. Berwick Workshop on Issues Related to Accountable Care Organizations. Baltimore, MD, October 5, 2010. Available at: http://www.healthreformgps.org/wp-content/uploads/he10062010_berwick.pdf.

8. CMS Office of Legislation. Medicare Accountable Care Organizations Shared Savings Program. Available at: www.cms.gov/OfficeofLegislation/Downloads/AccountableCare Organization.pdf.

9. Spending, Use Of Services, Prices, And Health In 13. Available at: http://www.com-monwealthfund.org/publications/issue-briefs/2015/oct/us-health-car.

Chapter 3

Negotiating Managed Care Contracts

Negotiation

We all know that the key to success in negotiation is leverage. Physicians do not become proactive unless they see that it affects their total income. Most physicians do not recognize an advantage, and they sometimes do not use it appropriately when going into negotiations. Unfortunately, many managed care payers have created a situation where they have either become hated by the physician community or vilified in the healthcare press. Most payers have very reduced physician reimbursement, and they have been able to increase their insurance premiums without increasing physician premiums. They have also placed a lot of red tape around the possibility of the physician renewing or renegotiating their contract. Therefore, it is hard to understand the benefit of negotiating with a health maintenance organization (HMO). The best thing to do, if possible, is to negotiate from scratch. It is much harder to renegotiate an existing contract than it is to negotiate a new agreement. When starting negotiations, we need to understand what the market share and physician practice area are, and what the anticipated market share over the next two years will be. How does the plan intend to secure this market share? Which employees are going to sign up for the program? Which other physicians and physician medical specialties are also participating in the providing-plan? Which hospitals will participate in the program? If a physician is not able to deliver a certain number of patients, the program is not working, and a negotiation needs to be initiated. Think about leverage, and how you can use it in physician support. If a contract is found to be unacceptable, you should renegotiate it. To do that, a physician should analyze the reimbursement rate.

Locate the Reimbursement Rate

The reimbursement that allows the practice of 20–30 Current Procedural Terminology (CPT) codes and objectives to identify a service with steep discounts should be identified. Since managed care payers have adopted the Medicare payment system for the reimbursement of physician providers, it is also a good idea to review the current compensation under Medicare. Reasonable managed care rates based on relative value units (RVUs) are as follows:

1. Evaluation and management service 130–145 of Medicare. All other functions 150–170 of Medicare.
2. Application of the cost-benefit ratio to the process. The cost is then based on the average value of the CPT code.

Once the hospital procedures have been determined, the results of the evaluation and negotiation of the managed care contract can be used. We need to keep in mind that this result may also be used to estimate the practice/member/monthly cost for evaluation and a new contract. When we are trying to re-contract, we do not think about legal issues. Conducting a financial analysis gives some legal problems; therefore, it is essential to engage a healthcare attorney to review the contract and make suggestions for changes before entering into a negotiation.[1]

Independent Practice Association

To ensure leverage by a group of physicians, most of the physicians will attempt to form an independent practice association (IPA). This is a state nonprofit corporation and limited liability company that brings physicians together to negotiate a contract. It can use independent messengers, it can be a costly model receiving capitation from a managed care payer, or it can be a mixed model IPA, usually for a fee for a service contract. Members typically agree and lower the service fee for the deal. Many IPAs are formed to obtain risk-sharing contracts. The leveraged figure alone will not guarantee the contract, although it gets you to the negotiating table where you must demonstrate other benefits to leverage the payer. It is essential, when you do create an association, to consider antitrust law. The government will always be concerned about organized physician activities and will scrutinize any multiple provider networks. The government discourages anti-competitive behavior and, more importantly, physicians organizing themselves with the sole objective of driving up healthcare costs. The government, in general, will focus on the following seven principles:

1. Integration
2. Joint pricing and marketing

3. Market share
4. Competitive effect
5. Exclusive area
6. Exclusion of providers
7. Efficiency

Leverages

In the past, there have been examples of people coming together and being sued by the government. The problem is that most IPAs could never threaten the payer; they cannot terminate a contract unless they have to, and they have to watch what they put in writing. A qualified attorney should be involved in this process.

The important points of leverage are

1. *Number*: a group of physicians, IPAs, Procurement Orders (POs), etc.
2. *Geography*: competition lacking where there are few physicians
3. *Volume*: 20% or more of patients from a particular insurance provider
4. *Quality*: a good metric to highlight
5. *Termination agreement*: the physician can stop the contract if it is not a lock-in contract

Make sure that each physician makes this decision individually, and not as part of the group, and make sure that you have some leverage; otherwise, you risk losing all of your income from that type of insurance. In the final subsection of this chapter, the negotiation capitation contract is discussed.

HMO

HMO is an interesting area, and it is becoming more populous since it has come to play a role in healthcare. Money is typically allocated monthly for each patient in practice, and is multiplied for the number of patients treated to calculate the amount of money that will be received from insurance.

The problem with this type of contract is that there is a price risk, and it should therefore be ensured that there is a market below the practice cost of doing business.

1. *Market risk*: The HMO might have to reduce treatment to maintain the market share.
2. *Selection risk*: Should a patient that is very sick, young, and so forth be selected?
3. *Partner risk*: Your partner needs to do the same job.
4. Regulatory Risk.

All of these risks can impact the profitability of any capitation arrangement. The problem with capitation is that you have a certain amount of money for patients, so the more they utilize the service, the less money the practice makes. It is important to have a mixed population of younger patients, who you know are going to come into the office less, and older patients, who will utilize more of your services. It is very important is to obtain an exclusive contract with the payer. Contracts are typically for one year, but there are some HMOs that give long-term contracts.

It is important to know what the market share is and what it is going to be in a few years. Make sure that the contract is not exclusive, and then you can work without an HMO. It is also important to know which services are included, such as labs, x-rays etc.

You should also know whether there are bonuses available. Second, you should know how the bonuses will be divided. The percentage of the bonus is typically between 25% and 50%. Most bonuses are turned into shared risk, meaning that the bonus will be divided with a physician, but if there is a loss, the physician will have to pay the HMO back. It is important to determine which one is in the contract, which partner you are going to share the bonus with, and whether another physician is included in the HMO to know if you can achieve the bonus.

Note

1. Reed Tinsley. *Managed Care Contracting: Successful Negotiation Strategies*. AMA Publication. 2001.

Suggested Reading

1. Michael A. Fauman. *Negotiating Managed Care: A Manual for Clinicians*. Washington, DC: American Psychiatric Association Publishing, 2008.
2. Robert D. Keene and Fred F. Naus. *Negotiating Manage Care Contracts*. New York, NY: McGraw-Hill, 1994.

Chapter 4

Hospital Supply Chain and Cost Containment

Quest for Excellence and Cost Containment

The supply chain is a quest for excellence based on value analysis (VA). VA is centered on evidence-based criteria from physician and organizational input, which in turn will support or deny the purchase of new technology.

The supply-chain process ensures that the physician is involved since it has been shown that physician-oriented decisions enhance patient outcomes, thus increasing organizational resources and potential savings.

The physician can see how the product can and needs to be used.

To obtain the best results from the VA, it is imperative to set up a value analysis committee (VAC). This panel will evaluate the clinical and financial side of the product, comprises physicians and nonphysicians, and can call experts on an ad hoc basis if the product requires further evaluation by clinical users.

For instance, for a clinical scenario involving a drug-eluting stent (DES), a cardiologist is at the center of the decision. Lawn-care services, best office supplies, paper shredding, etc. need a purely financial decision, not clinical expertise.

In general, the operative expenses of a hospital should be around 60%. Hospital supply-chain expenses are around 40%.

The goal is to limit these last expenses. Industry best-practice guidelines recommend the complete turnover of an operating room's inventory ten times annually. The value of some hospital inventories is close to or more than USD$2.6 million without consignment items. Here are some other numbers:

- 30%–40% of supply expenses are physician-preferred items
- 10% of the total operating cost

- Preference items may or may not
  - Be linked to outcomes/performance
  - Have an associated contracted purchase price (be on a contract)
  - Be based on evidence
  - Be fully reimbursed
- A successful VA will address both clinical and financial issues by reviewing all available research and payer reimbursement

Goal of the Supply Chain

The goal is to implement a management strategy that will increase usage of the available material by meeting physician preferences and avoiding buying material that sits on the shelf forever. This can, by itself, decrease costs by 34%. Another item, which requires having the physicians on board, is to reduce the individual issues that account for 10% of supply-chain expenses, if not more.

Items may or may not be linked to outcomes and performance processing. Therefore, the contract for the purchasing pricing should be based on evidence. This is the role of the VAC, where the physicians and administration need to work together.

- All products must *meet* the clinical needs
- The cost of a product is made up of more than just the unit price. Other factors that contribute to a product's cost-effectiveness include:
  a. *Quality*—quality is a composite criterion for performance.
  b. *Effectiveness*—how well an item meets its intended purpose.
  c. *Costs*—cost will include the financial impact of the acquisition, holding, stocking, handling, disposal, processing, and utilization.
  d. *Storage/space*—the need for ample room.
  e. *Packaging*—optimal packaging and ease of use.
  f. *Availability*—the product will be available when needed.
  g. *Operation*—consider the impact of using the product and system capabilities.
  h. *Education and training* – consider these requirements.
  i. *Safety*—the item will comply with all hospital Joint Commission on Accreditation of Healthcare Organizations (JCAHO) and Occupational Safety and Health Administration (OSHA) regulations.
  j. *Service and repair*—vendor provision of service and repair time will meet the user's needs.

Physician Role

Seventy-two percent of the VCA's decision is physician-oriented. So, to improve this figure, the material should be standardized. The revenue cycle can be improved down to 52% by implementing evidence-based medicine and research, meeting with physicians from each specialty.

How can we engage physicians without telling them what to do?

Three areas with the most opportunity in the future to gain physician trust and buy-in are

1. Engaging the physician in the development of a supply-chain strategic plan with clear goals and accountabilities.
2. Sharing data and reporting with physicians to increase awareness of costs and outcomes.
3. Developing physician awareness through training and education.

The VAC provides the formal collaborative approach to do this. It is like building an algorithm, but for supply purposes. The interdisciplinary team can include an overview of the supply and service requested, which will ensure the understanding of the product. This will consist of the clinical need by an expert physician. This process will ensure the buy-in and support of the physician.

Forcing products down the physician's throat is not the way to go since it will create hatred, although many hospitals are still learning this.

The physician should be able to:

■ Evaluate all vendor solicitations and negotiations
■ Take responsibility for the implementation of pricing and product changes
■ Collaborate with finance to prepare business cases to support the analysis of requests for new products or technology
■ Coordinate interaction and communication with contracting and the Group Purchasing Organization (GPO)

If the physician is not happy with the hospital supply, he or she will order outside the formulary, and the contracted amounts (medication or instrument) can create an increase in costs.

Consistent types of medical service or supply will then represent the standard and decreased costs and will also give the hospital the chance of better contracts with the specific company.

The Physician Struggle

Unfortunately, when purchasing is done from a national office and items are sent to the different hospitals it owns around the country, the physician mostly has no say and no power, and that creates animosity.

Supply chain committees at the local level are powerless, and even if they meet the decision, they need to go to regional and national levels. This needs to be apparent to physicians, who think that their input is essential and do not understand that, at the end of the day, it will not have any effect.

There must be room for local hospitals to have the opportunity to ask their physicians for their opinion and to proceed with change if needed, but most of the time it is like fighting Godzilla.

Physicians need to have transparent associations with the company, showing that they want the product for the good of all and not because they have connections with the company.

The hospital needs to be more transparent in its interactions with the contracting group, the group purchasing organization, etc., showing that they do not receive a financial kick-back out of the process and can provide the best supply possible for the best price.

A steering committee should be active in each hospital, with the chief of each department, the director of staff, and the administrator participating.

Physicians need to provide input to the steering committee by looking into material management purchasing and then product implementation, with the supervision of the purchaser by the board.

The VAC should support this interaction by establishing effective communication with the steering committee and using budget adjustment in planning. This can be the result of cost-saving notices of product changes to a user providing a progress report to the organization or an approved policy and procedure related to product authorization. The VAC needs to give final approval to value analysis decisions that will affect effective costs to meet clinical needs.

The VAC is also in charge of controlling the access of the vendors to the hospital. Vendor control needs to comply with the joint commission. The joint commission require that vendors in procedural areas can prove their product/service competency.

Suggested Reading

1. www.amazonbusiness.com/hospital/supply-sourcing.
2. Jacqueline LaPointe. 2016, August 5. Exploring the Role of Supply Chain Management in Healthcare. *RevCycle Intelligence*. Available at: https://revcycleintelligence.com/news/exploring-the-role-of-supply-chain-management-in-healthcare.
3. 10 Trends in Hospital Supply Chain Management. 2014, April 30. *Becker's Hospital Review*. Available at: https://www.beckershospitalreview.com/supply-chain/10-trends-in-hospital-supplychain-management.html.
4. Detlef Schwartimg, Jad Bitar, Yash Arya, and Thomas Pfeiffer. The Transformative Hospital Supply Chain: Balancing Costs with Quality. *Booz & Co.* https://www.strategyand.pwc.com/media/uploads/Strategyand-Transformative-Hospital-Supply-Chain.pdf.

Chapter 5

Quality Crisis

The Health System as an Industry

Health-system economics have inflated and deflated in the last 30 years. Some hospitals in the 1980s established an internal agency to regulate their flow and to review requests for the hospital's facilities and equipment. State agencies were created to promote and embrace the facility charge. The problem with this plan was that the hospital became an industry with similar settings and, like other companies, the terminology was directed toward a service and a product. The product involved many variables such as patients of different ages and different diseases to treat, which made it difficult for hospitals to obtain enough information to make intelligent decisions. At that point, healthcare paid for the service; therefore, there were few incentives to control the cost. Some believed that the best way to obtain efficiency might be to design a simple reimbursement system, one that would encourage healthcare providers to cover the costs when they treated the patients. By making healthcare providers share the costs and inefficiencies, the hospital tried to implement its new system. Before 1984, most insurance companies paid out through their bill charge, less the discount figure. Many Medicare and Medicaid plans paid costs. The hospitals reimbursed actual costs to make a commercial profit but did not take into consideration that the easiest way to increase profit was a cost-plus contract.

Hospital Health Plans

A significant revolution came with the consolidation of hospital institute incorporation chains. This was a difficult time for many hospitals and administrators who had grown accustomed to autonomy and, in some cases, the lack of accountability within the entire system. The second revolution took place in the 1980s with the introduction of the prospective payment system. Cost reimbursement enforced rules on healthcare providers.

In the 1990s, more and more providers assumed an insurance role, bypassing the insurance company and contracting directly with the employers for the provision of comprehensive service. The provider understood the economic risks of insurance because of the market share. Prospective payment placed a limit on global hospital revenues; it had state-by-state payment limits. The only way for hospitals to increase revenue was to capture this operation. Therefore, hospitals started to obtain health plans by dictating to employees which physician they must see to receive the maximum discount and by controlling hospital admission partners and participating physicians. The second issue for the hospital was cost control. One of the most effective organizations providing insurance is the Health Maintenance Organization (HMO).

Focus on Quality

The sole focus should be on quality. This is where the healthcare industry is today. Several factors emphasize quality, including:

1. Choice of physician and hospital mandated by their employers
2. Increased access to health information through the Internet
3. Procedures have shown an improvement in products through total quality management and continuous quality improvement.[1]

Where do we obtain this information to conform to the standard of care?

1. Medical records
2. Business office
3. Physician's office
4. Hospital

Quality Care

Quality has always been the goal of every physician. Nowadays, every single healthcare organization and/or hospital has a program related to quality assurance and improvement.

Metrics are routinely collected, many of which are required by federal and state regulations. Physician leaders are now working with organizations to share the value of quality, improve quality, measure performance, etc.

Physicians are meeting with other physicians to try to comply with the benchmarks. Although quality care has always been provided, it has never been as focused on quality as it is now.

Quality is the basis of every single strategy in healthcare organization and is justified as it improves patients' health, reduces costs, and ensures the sustainability of the healthcare organization. The only, and critical, measure of quality has been the review of cases by physicians at morbidity and mortality conferences, but this is insufficient and needs to be more standardized.

Healthcare is becoming a more patient-centric business since healthcare organizations recognize that quality is directly correlated to the financial return and the need for saving on expenditure, which again will increase and sustain the financial stability of any healthcare organization.

Quality starts with people. Respect for the patient by the physician and respect for the physician by the administration will ensure the best adequate care and the best patient-centered care.

These outcomes can only be achieved through the empowerment of the physician as a leader and placing him or her charge of controlling quality in the hospital. Quality requires knowledge of performance improvement on the clinical side of patient care. Only the physician can provide these components.

Patients' View of Quality is Different

What does the patient see? The patient has the *perception of quality*. For patients, this is usually secondary to their attitudes, beliefs, and opinions of their physician or the hospital or for treatment they receive in the hospital. Patients can get upset because their coffee is cold, but might not comment on the healthcare team. They therefore mix perception with results.

A friendly physician can lead to good scores by patients on quality issues, as most patients do not understand the complexity of medicine. They know if they are doing well or not, but might not realize that they can have adverse results, not because the physician is incompetent, but because they have neglected their own health and expect the physician to be a magician and solve their problems with a magic wand.

Furthermore, some patients don't understand their conditions.

It is essential for physicians to set specific and clear expectations of care to help the patient to understand the physician's care plan, improve the physician-patient relationship, and give the patient the perspective of better quality.

This the *appreciative* quality, which represents what the patient understands about the physician.

But how can we measure quality and what the physician needs to focus on? The physician must track metrics. Of course, mortality and morbidity, the functional status of the patient, the timing of antibiotic treatment, appropriate care, access to care, infection rates, etc., represent the basis of clinical quality. Quality issues can change, even within the same organization.

How can healthcare organizations and physicians adjust to the changing faces of quality? There is no question that issues about quality are dynamic issues. Quality has never been a static issue in the sense that has been changing year by year. Every year there is a new publication, new discovery, or new technology that can be applied to improve quality. Therefore, the expectation is always that quality can be improved.

To achieve this, we need physicians to undergo continuing medical education and learn all the things that can help to improve the quality of patient care.

We also need to break the barriers of "silo quality care" where each physician applies different metrics and different publication data are presenting challenges to the standardization of care across the healthcare system. Physicians practice in different ways, but all need to agree on the same type of care.

In medicine, physicians or surgeon can achieve excellent results in different ways, which is good but can create more confusion.

Better standardization of quality goals should be implemented. How? By a change in culture. Cultural changes based on patterns of behavior within an organization require either changing the core value of the organization or continuing to improve the existent core value.

Continuous Improvement

What type of culture is needed? One of continuous improvement that achieves uncompromised quality. A hospital culture that favors roundtable discussion and the collection of objective data-based evidence.

We need to eliminate organizations that decide to change strategy and quality based on administrative leaders with the support of senior physician leaders who have lost touch with the clinical scenario or have become aligned with the social business, forgetting the culture of caring for the patient.

Organizations need to question themselves to create an environment where a continuous process of analyzing data and every performance is in place. The physician evaluating quality should establish the committee. This should be quality at its best, since physicians from different specialties are not the best to judge others. The goal is to seek the opportunity to improve and review patient care and the quality that will bring success to the organization.

The Physician as a Manager

Healthcare is continually changing, and physicians busy updating themselves in the medical field find themselves with two roles:

1. To be an excellent physician
2. To be a good manager of the practice

Most private and academic practices are becoming businesses, and the physicians are becoming businesspeople. Physicians today need to understand the business aspects of becoming good managers.

The first thing needed to run an efficient business is good employees, but is that enough? Is that the only requirement for success? One thing physicians learn in medical school is always to rethink and doubt the initial diagnosis to be sure they reach the correct diagnosis. It should be the same in business. It seems that most things are done better when the rules are reassessed and reconsidered. The goal is not just to look at breaking the rules, but to reframe the aptitude so that it can be adapted and done in a new way.

A new physician should be a manager of his/her office. Managers need to build a robust and productive workplace and seek feedback. This feedback can be obtained using questionnaires. No one likes one-on-one feedback because people are afraid of being punished for their comments, but everyone should be willing to fill out an anonymous survey. Moreover, there are tools on the market that can help physicians to assess their employees using open, written questions so that they can express their feelings, even if they are not anonymous. One of the best examples of these tools is in the book *First, Break All the Rules*,[2] which reports the power of twelve questions to assess employees. Some of these questions are interesting because you can ask your employees what they think about their job and they give feedback, not only about how they feel about the situation, but also how they feel about the workplace and how they would like to improve it. One of the most critical things missed is the fact that some employees have much better ideas on how to improve the workplace than the people managing the workplace because they do not have to operate it on a daily basis. This is true in healthcare as well, and physicians should therefore have a stronger voice.

Notes

1. Health Care Quality. (n.d.). *Wikipedia*. Available at: https://en.wikipedia.org/wiki/Health_care_quality.
2. Marcus Buckingham and Curt Coffman. *First, Break All the Rules*. New York, NY: Simon and Schuster, 1999.

Suggested Reading

1. E. Andrew Ballas. 2016, July 21. The Untold Crisis in Medical Research. *The Washington Monthly*. Available at: https://washingtonmonthly.com/2016/07/21/the-untold-crisis-in-medical-research/.

2. USDHHS. 2003. Addressing the New Health Care Crisis: Reforming the Medical Litigation System to Improve the Quality of Health Care. Available at: https://aspe.hhs.gov/basic-report/addressing-new-health-care-crisis-reforming-medical-litigation-system-improve-quality-health-care.
3. USDHHS. 2002. Confronting the New Health Care Crisis: Improving Health Care Quality and Lowering Costs By Fixing Our Medical Liability System. Available at: https://aspe.hhs.gov/basic-report/confronting-new-health-care-crisis-improving-health-care-quality-and-lowering-costs-fixing-our-medical-liability-system.
4. Richard P. Lofgren, Michael Karpf, Jay Perman and Courtney M. Higdon. The U.S. healthcare system is in crisis: Implications for academic medical centers and their missions. *Academic Medicine* 81(8): 713–720, 2006.

Chapter 6

Ethics and Deontology

What Are Ethics and Deontology?

Family, religion, life, experiences, historical perspective, personal training, and education are the basis of our ethical principles. Freud[1] suggested the line of conduct of combining self-effacement, self-sacrifice, compassion, and intensity of action.

Deontology is the way people judge the morality and the actions of others based on set requirements. Initially, people learn the rules within their family structure. Philosophers have helped to generate a greater understanding of ethics and the making of regulations. In 1930, C.D. Broad[2] described the "five types of ethical theory" in his book, reinforcing that it is our duty and obligation to obey codes of conduct and that we are responsible for our actions. This is how the word "consequentialism" was derived. So, if morals and duty exist, a significant judgment of those actions is always behind them.

Immanuel Kant[3] expressed the concept of morality as the individual's duty to do the right thing. An adverse outcome, as a product of a wrong moral choice, is based on the motive of the person and not on the result. This serves to underline that the highest good is for everybody, keeping in mind that that which is good for everybody is good for society.

When something is good only in and of itself, it does not have morality. Intelligence, pleasure, and perseverance aren't merely moral by themselves if they aren't good for everybody. Happiness has no moral qualification. Goodwill is the moral action that is correct for all.

As Kant wrote, wrong actions that are motivated by goodwill for all are still considered moral.

The remainder of Kant's philosophy includes the following:

1. Act toward a universal good
2. Treat others like family, with a simple and positive mean
3. Act as you feel would be best for humanity

There is no absolute right or absolute wrong. There are intentions and actions that lead to consequences. Even a lie could be useful if the motive is the good of all.

Deontology, Not Religion

Deontology is not a religion; it does not follow God's commandments but is a way of behaving that is set in our society. Unfortunately, deontology has been influenced by religious interests on some occasions.

In 2007, Frances Kamm[4] published the book *Intricate Ethics*, in which she described new theories. She started with the premise that it is wrong to harm a person. Her point was to explain the relative nature of morality.

We have to make the right decision all of the time with the goal of keeping deontology and ethical principles in mind; this is the suggestion of Iain King[5] in his book *How to Make Right Decisions and Be Right All the Time*.

The morality of our actions has implications, which is slightly different than the vision of Kant and Kamm.

Traditional deontology and ethical theories are based on consequentialism. They focus on doing well for the most significant number of people.

Moral Codes

The appropriate response to ethical concerns is a clarification of the values held by people and by organizations. If not revisited frequently, a moral code can be forgotten or strayed from.

Moral principles should form the basis of any business; a framework should be in place before launching a business or any practice in the hospital or private sectors.

A good starting point is to write down the ten most important values that will guide the practice in an ideal society.

Change is tough. Where there is a conflict of interest or conflict of ethics, ethical principles of moral courage must be discussed. Constraints are imposed by daily practice, by corporate structure, by politics, by authority; effectively, an unhealthy culture can creep in. A good organization should represent the definite answer and not the constriction.

It is crucial for a system to frame its purpose in such a way that the whole organization can follow certain principles. Therefore, a consistent ethical code needs to be applied using this method for the customers and the people that form the system. This will help to ensure constant discernment regarding greater mutual understanding and organization.

Safety First

The temptation to ensure ethical compromise will always be part of the community. Temptation can prove a test of one's values and even of one's faith. It may sound religious, but all religions deal with attraction as a tool for strengthening one's faith.

We lack the consistency of ethical frameworks established at the administrative level. Therefore, it is difficult for employees to do the right thing. If we build a moral structure for our practice, if we learn how to deal with ethical issues, we can support employees and gain the loyalty of customers. Without such a clear structure, it becomes difficult for most employees to carry out their duties efficiently.

Management do not always know what to do, and most will react vehemently to ethical issues.

This approach will destroy the practice, the hospital, and the systems since the professional growth of all within the organization is directly connected with the moral and ethical conduct of those in charge. The employees look up to management, and react accordingly. Three strikes and we lose.

These principles are not about the bylaws of the business. They are about the boundaries within which the industry can safely grow. We hear the phrase "safety first" frequently. But how often do we think of it in an ethical framework? Only by working toward the good of all will we achieve success. Only through consistent ethical practices, as per Immanuel Kant, can business and a method grow and prosper.

Solving Medical Ethics Issues

How can we address the moral problems? One answer: by clarification of your values. At times, we all lose sight of the main road and need to stop and reassess our values.

Most of the time, respect for human life, honesty, and fairness are chosen. If you can make sensible choices, then your employees can do that too. If you discover flaws in this process, then you have a problem; perhaps your customers have identified the problem before you, and that is why you are losing them.

Principles or moral courage are significant because when you have a conflict of ethics, only your courage can enable you to discuss it.

Impeccable moral ethics is essential under pressure in the corporate structure, authority, and politics. At times, many businesses make unethical requests, and saying "no" could pose a risk.

Ethics for All

Ethics should be introduced in every school. This would empower employees to make better decisions about their roles. A greater understanding of ethics can help individuals in administrative positions.

Each of us comes with the ethics and morals learned at home. A culture of safety should be instilled in each person before he or she enters the workplace. Only through a consistent ethical code and the teaching of strict deontology might we be able to create this culture of safety.

We must provide people with a conceptual tool to navigate through the ethical issues that they will encounter in clinical practice. Necessary steps need to be taken during their training that focus on discussion, examples, and fundamental principles. A proper learning experience should encourage people to explore and develop moral ethics. They can build their boundaries, and most importantly, they will be not afraid to say "no" because they know where to draw the line.

We realize that it is challenging to implement ethical principles in a business where all that is important is time and money. On the other hand, what hospital owners might not understand is that customers will also eventually be affected by the morality of the hospital business and their bosses.

Only by setting ethical boundaries can a business grow and flourish; fraud, politics, rumors, favoritism, mistreatment of employees, and irresponsible management of finances will soon become apparent, and the industry will fall like a "house of cards."[6]

Notes

1. R.N. Kaul. Freud's Contribution to Ethical Theory. *Psychoanal Review*, 51: 612–618, 1965.
2. C.D. Broad. *Five Types of Ethical Theory*. New York: Harcourt, Brace and Co., 1930.
3. Immanuel Kant. *Groundwork of the Metaphysic of Morals*. New York, NY: Harper and Row Publishers, 1964.
4. Frances M. Kamm. *Intricate Ethics Rights, Responsibilities, and Permissible Harm, Rights, Responsibilities, and Permissible Harm*. New York, NY: Oxford University Press, 2007.
5. Iain King. *How to Make Right Decisions and Be Right All the Time*. London, UK: Bloomsbury Publishing, 2008.
6. Eldo E. Frezza and Gianmarco E. Frezza. Ethics and deontology in business. *Austin Journal of Business Administration and Management*, 1(2): 1007, 2017; http://austin-publishinggroup.com/business-administration-and-management/fulltext.

Suggested Reading

1. Tom L. Beauchamp. *Philosophical Ethics: An Introduction to Moral Philosophy*, Second Edition. New York, NY: McGraw-Hill, 1991.
2. A. Flew. Consequentialism. In *A Dictionary of Philosophy*, Second Edition. New York, NY: St Martin's, 1979.
3. R.G. Olson. Deontological Ethics. In Paul Edwards (Ed.), *The Encyclopedia of Philosophy*. London, UK: Collier Macmillan, 1967.
4. W.D. Ross. *The Right and the Good*. Oxford, UK: Clarendon Press, 1930.
5. T.A. Salzman. *Deontology and Teleology: An Investigation of the Normative Debate in Roman Catholic Moral Theology*. Leuven, Belgium: Leuven University Press, 1995.
6. B.N. Waller. *Consider Ethics: Theory, Readings, and Contemporary Issues*. New York, NY: Pearson Longman, 2005.

PHYSICIAN
STRUGGLES

Chapter 7

The Economics of Being a Doctor in the US

Cost of US Medical Schools vs Rest of the World

In this chapter I will dissect the different stages to becoming a doctor in the US, how much it costs to attend medical school, and how many more hours US doctors work than in other countries.

Medical School

First, let me start with medical school. We are importing doctors from other countries, which has been the norm for many years. Since medical schools outside the US are less expensive, students who wish to become physicians have more opportununties and possibilties to become one by attending medical school outside the US. To offset the cost of an excellent medical education, NYU recently launched a program designed to provide free admission to medical school predicated on tuition and living expenses of more that $100,000 a year. All told, by going to school in the US, a medical student spends about $50,000 for each of the four years undergraduate, which is equal to $200,000 and then $60,000 a year for medical school, which comes to $240,000. So every graduate in this country who becomes an MD spends around $440,000 to go to school, plus room and board. Moreover, they have to pay to take the MCAT (an exam that allows students to apply for medical school) and the USMLE which is an exam that helps them go from being just a graduate to having a valid license in the US. The USMLE is composed of four parts, all which have a separate fee. Taking both exams costs between $1000 and $2000. So when it is all said and done, a student in the US, who graduates and officially becomes a doctor going into a residency program, starts their career with a deficit of more than $500,000 to be paid when they start working.

If you take a medical school graduate from a foreign country (and I know this because I am a graduate from a foreign country), the cost of attending medical school is between $1000 and $3000 a year. The length of the program outside the US is six years between college and medical school, not the eight years required in the US. Therefore, if you calculate even the highest, most expensive school, let's say the $3000 a year, multiplied by six years, the total medical school expense is around $18,000. There is only one state exam that costs less than $1000, so rounding it all off, a student attending a university outside the US can graduate from medical school for about $20,000. So why would anybody send their children to medical school in the US and spend half a million dollars to do so, when they can go to another country, including England, and come out of school with only a $20,000 deficit?

Of course, we are talking about state schools that, even outside the US, are more affordable than private schools, which can cost a lot of money. For example, let's say you want to go to Cambridge University in the UK. Cambridge is a very well-known academic institution and probably the oldest university in the world. If you want to go there to study political science or something else, you spend perhaps $30,000 for undergraduate college and then the expense for medical school and so forth. But if a student goes directly to medical school instead, they embark on a six-year program, and even if they go to a private medical school in England, Italy, or France, it could cost $30,000 a year for six years or $180,000. That is to attend a private school, compared to $500,000 that the average student in the US will have to pay to go to medical school.

How Much Money Do U.S. Doctors Earn Compared to the Hours They Work?

After medical school, the new doctors enter residency programs, and residents work a lot of hours. When I was a resident, I worked 120 hours a week. Now, I work about 80 hours a week as a physician. The corporations that own hospitals around the country pay the physician for a 40-hour work week, plus extra if they are on call. The average week in Europe is 36 hours. In France, it is about 34 hours. The difference between the physician in Europe and a physician in the US is that after the physician in Europe finishes his 40-hour week, he's done, his work week is done, and he goes home. In the US, it is never just a 40-hour work week because physicians in the US are always available for their patients. In Europe, when you finish the shift another physician comes in and starts their shift. In Europe, it becomes a shift job for the physician, not a 24/7, 365-days-a-year job as in the US.

So, let's take an example. Let's say that we bring the same concept they have in Europe to the US, which is a 36-hour work week. So, if I am a surgeon and I am on call for 24 hours, it means a day and a half and I'm on call all day. Healthcare is not an office job. This is a 24-hour job. The patient does not get sick when we have office hours; they get sick whenever they get sick. If I am a physician in Europe, the physician is on call for 24 hours and in the morning, you go home. You come back the day after to do a 6-hour shift or 12-hour shift. I take one 24-hour shift and one half-day shift, and I am done. The other four days are covered by another physician. To illustrate, you need four doctors to cover services for a week. If you pay each of them $100,000 a year, that $400,000 for four physicians instead of one reduces the risk of physician burnout.

I might take three night shifts, 7 p.m. to 7 a.m. Or I may take three day shifts, 7 a.m. to 7 p.m. It doesn't matter, I only work three shifts or three days a week; the other four days are free. I am okay with that because they are going to pay us less, but hey, we have four days off.

I remember one year practicing in the US. I probably had a total of five days off. Physicians in Europe have the opportunity to take a three-month holiday versus in the US where the typical vacation is 28 days. In Europe, you can take up to three months of sick leave or to recuperate from an illness. In the US, you typically have five days. Between the time required to see patients and be on call, plus administrative responsibilities (patient records, etc.) and the typical holiday pay, shouldn't physicians in the US be paid more to compensate them for their time?

Healthcare Is Not a Shift Job for Physicians

I think that most people talk about healthcare as a shift job. It's about time that we talk about healthcare as an entirely different type of situation in this country because as a physician, we take care of patients, so if the patient doesn't sleep, the physician can't sleep! Patients are not a car. They are not animals. People don't always get sick at convenient times during normal work hours. We as physicians, need to be there when the patient is sick, not by scheduled hours. If you want to change the whole system and part of that change is a decreased salary for physicians, then physicians are going to become hourly workers. If this is the case, then the patient can't say, "But you are a doctor. You are supposed to take care of me because that's what you went to medical school for." What patients don't understand is that physicians have families to support, children to send to college, and expenses just as they do. Even doctors need money. They cannot just work for nothing. Physician reimbursement is getting more complicated every day. With the expense of current technologies, it harder than ever for physicians today to make a living.

Reimbursement Issues for Physicians: The 33% Rule

The last issue I want to tackle is the reimbursement. If you work in Europe, you work for the federal government. Therefore you always get paid. It is like having Medicare patients all the time. You can work in the private sector to supplement income which means you get paid before you perform the surgery. In the US, one-third of patients do not pay because they do not have money or insurance. One-third of patients have health insurance, but the insurance companies scrutinize every claim and can deny payment and sometimes they don't get paid. So only one-third of patients in the US pay bills from the physician. If you think about it, the physician as a professional fills the only job in the US that does not get paid for a service before providing the service itself. Try going to a lawyer and saying, "Let's go to trial first and then I'll pay you." I don't think the lawyer will even open the door for you. Why should the physician? Healthcare is not a business. Healthcare is talking about soul, talking about emotions, talking about people. So let's stop thinking about healthcare as any other job and pay the doctor appropriately when they provide patient care when their patients need it. If you're a physician in Europe, you are paid by the federal government, but in the US, your income is dependent on a patient's ability to pay or you're at the mercy of the insurance companies or federally funded programs. In the early part of their careers, physicians in the US start practicing with huge medical school debt and struggle daily to make ends meet. And many times, their salaries don't match the hours they devote to patient care. Things have to change in order to encourage more students to become physicians.

Astronomical Malpractice Insurances

The last comment is about malpractice insurance. In this country, malpractice insurance costs are astronomical. Malpractice insurance is not paid in other countries, but because this country has a litigious leaning, physicians must have malpractice insurance to defend against frivolous lawsuits brought by people who think that by suing the doctor they can collect money that they would never make by working every day. But it is not the doctor's fault that some people have no idea how valuable a physician's services are until they need care. If people who are not in the healthcare field could follow a physician just for 2–3 days, then they could appreciate the physician's job and understand the money that a physician earns to practice medicine in this country.

Suggested Reading

Dean Baker on Politico, October 2017. https://www.politico.com/agenda/story/2017/10/25/doctors-salaries-pay-disparities-000557

https://www.quora.com/What-are-the-differences-in-salary-between-USA-Australia-UK-as-a-GP-doctor

https://theincidentaleconomist.com/wordpress/physician-fees-and-salaries-in-the-us-and-other-countries/

https://www.reddit.com/r/medicine/comments/3ala5m/salaries_for_doctors_in_the_uk_are_a_joke/

Chapter 8

The Fear: Financial Report

The Physician's Fear

Financial evaluation is a fear for all physicians, who are concerned about finding themselves trapped in numbers, line reports, etc. We can hire somebody to do it for us. However, if you have an understanding of the issue, you can have better control of your practice. Therefore, try here to approach the subject and make it easy (if that is possible!) to understand.

What Does Cash Flow Mean?

Cash flow refers to the amount of cash that moves in and out of your bank or office account, but it does not give the depth of the business. A company gets bashed on its cash flow, but many other parameters need to be evaluated 'to optimize cash flow or to better regulate it.

The Financial Statement

The *financial statement*, in general, refers to the complete set of accounts including the balance sheet, income statement, and cash flow statements. Most of us can understand a cash flow statement. Cash flow reveals virtually nothing about the financial condition of the business. There are other monetary aspects that include the *accrual base accounting*, which states the correct timing of recording, revenue, and expenses. In one sense, the cash flow report takes the place of the profit performance report and financial condition report. The term *profit* seems to be generally avoided in most of the statements. The *income statement* is designed to be read in a step-wise manner. Each step is a deduction of one or more expenses. *Earning* means earnings before interest and tax (EBIT). The net income divided by the number of stocks shared is called *earning per share* (EPS). The sales revenue is a net value. The *operating expenses* are the expenses other than the cost of goods sold, after interest and income tax are reported.

Fee and Earnings

The *fee* is the portion of the original price of the long-term asset. *Interest expense* is the interest-bearing liability. Income taxes include both federal and state taxes. Each separate asset liability on the balance sheet is called an account. A line is drawn above the subtotal or total, indicating that a balance has been added. A double underline dictates the last of the month in the column. The double underscore below, net income, shows the last number in the column. The *accrual assets* are cash and other assets that will be converted into cash in an operative cycle. The *depreciation* is each period of usage bearing a share of the total cost of each fixed asset. *Liability* includes short-term liabilities and long-term liabilities. These include assets, but also other debts such as borrowed money. Liability has a claim on the assets of the business. It is imperative therefore to know what the liability is because not only can it be an asset, but it can also represent what the business owns. *Retaining earning* is not an asset. The above is most of the information that we need to know. The ability of managers to make a sale and control expenses, and therefore to earn a profit, is summarized in an *income statement*. The goal of management to manage the company's asset liabilities and prevent cash-outs. Beyond that, the business should move on to financial condition analysis and cash flow analysis.

In addition to the balance sheet and income statement, a basic financial statement is required to be included in a financial report outside of the business, which is the cash flow statement. A rather strict connection between the financial statements is the *income statement for the year*, balance sheet, and cash flow statement for the year. Extending credit to costs creates a cash inflow lag. The *accounts receivable balance* is the extend of this lag. Therefore, at the end of the tax cycle, there are some cash-receivable accounts that have not been cashed, and accordingly, which can be planned as an account receivable at the end of the year. The *average sale credit* determines the value of the accounts receivable.

Inventory

The inventory is the cost of all products sold to the customer during the year, but it also subtracts the value of goods sold from the sales revenue to give the gross margin, which is the first profit line. Therefore, you should know how much inventory you have and how much you can buy to determine your first profit margin.

How to Record Expenses

This can be done in four primary ways. One way is to *sort expenses* by when they are paid, and this makes sense, but it seems like there would be a full awareness if every dollar of operating costs were a dollar paid out. For many operating expenses, businesses cannot wait to record the expenditures until that payment is received. As soon as the liability is incurred, the cost amount should be recorded. The business should know the average time it takes to pay the short-term accounts payable. The average credit lag for a company would be around three weeks. The accounts payable should be recorded for expenses that have been paid by the end of the accounting year. There are other costs that are hidden. The accounts receivable and the price are paid before the tax cycle or at the beginning of the tax cycle, such as insurance, malpractice, probably taxes, and so forth. The business should have a prepaid *expense balance*, covering operating expenses. What other costs could a business have? We have depreciation of equipment, the house, the office, and everything we use. These are the so-called *fixed assets*. In a month, it is comparable to the fixed asset because that is the cost to the business of buying the fixed asset. Fixed assets are used for several years, but eventually they wear down like a truck, car, and so forth. It is interesting that the government allows you to report an accelerated depreciation, meaning that you can depreciate what you buy in the early part of the year more than in the later part of the year. For instance, it is interesting that the depreciation of a building is 39 years, even if a structure can be as old as 70 years. Amortization of a car is 5 years, even if the car lasts for 15 years. The question is that it seems like most of the fixed values sometimes get bigger and they do not retain the initial cost value.

The expenses that are not accounts payable are operative expenses and accrual operative expenses. Costs paid are recorded so that the full and correct charge is recognized when they should measure profit. To document these expenses, the company makes an entry in the liability account under accrued operative fees, which is a different liability from accounts payable. There are several other *accrual expenses* that need to be recorded at the end of the period such as accumulation of vacation, sick leave, interest on taxes, and so forth. What accounts should have is a gestation period of about 6 weeks before paying. What the net income is at this point is an accumulated deficit or some asset that can be covered by earnings that are not considered cash. The *earning* can be done as winning as the cash barrier or EPS, which is the net income divided by the number of stockholders. Only private companies have to report EPS at the bottom of their income statement.

Cash Flow

Under cash flow, which is the third primary part of the financial statement, we need to see the figure reported as cash. Despite the fact that most of the company and most of the investors look at a cash flow statement, it means quite little at the beginning because you have to consider the accounts receivable, the inventory, prepaid expenses, depreciation that is written down as a cost, the accounts payable, the accrual expenses, and the income tax payable. Increasing operative assets causes a decrease in cash flow from profit. Decreasing operating assets causes a decrease in cash flow for the benefit. Hence, there is a reverse effect of cash flow. Increased operative liability helps cash flow, but a decrease in operative responsibility results in a decrease in cash flow from profit. The *cash flow statement* focuses on cash flow from operative activities. This statement deserves as much attention and scrutiny as the income statement and balance sheet, although it is not too likely that a company making a profit could be headed for liquidity or solvency problems. *Profit* does not guarantee liquidity and solvency, however. Depreciation, a change in the operative asset, or decreased operative liability can affect the cash flow.

Data Manipulation

You can hide numbers, or you can use different measures to view numbers or decrease profits, using, for instance, the "last in, first out" (LIFO) method. This is used to steady cost inflation and maximize the cost of goods sold and expenses, and then to minimize profit. The first in, first out (FIFO) methods take the costs in of goods sold and expenses in chronological order. Another method was referring to the most reached center accusation (last in) and the oldest accusation (first out). The first in, first out method can, through cost inflation, minimize the cost of goods sold and expenses and maximize the gross margin. Why do we use this method? To minimize the taxable income. With LIFO, a business has the liberty to tolerate it below normal levels. Another method is the "lower cost for the market" (LCM), the purpose of which is to write down the inventory cost to recognize that the cost of replacement might fall below the recorded value of the product.

Ratio: Is It Right?

The *asset test ratio* or *quick ratio* relates only to cash, and fast assets converted into money. The *debt-to-equity ratio* is an indicator of whether the company is acting prudently or whether it has gone too far. The asset ratio is supposed to be 2 to 1. The debt–equity ratio is supposed to be around 1. The ratio is supposed to be above 2.2. The *timing to earn ratio*, which divides the operative earning by the interest expense, is supposed to be 12.6. The *return and sale ratio*, which is the profit divided by the sales revenue for the period, is supposed to be between 2 and 10. The *returns investment ratio*, which is a comparison with the amount of capital investment with the profit in return on equity ratio, is divided by the annual net income of the stockholder. The *return on equity ratio* is supposed to be around 21.6. The *return on asset ratio* is supposed to be approximately 23.1, and this reveals the operating earnings divided by the total asset. The return equity ratio is the net income divided by the number of stockholders, etc.

Final Thought

We should read financial statements because we should know what we are getting into if we are interested in the company. We need to know about the debts, work situation, process, and other situations such as bankruptcy, which is supposed to be disclosed. Comparing the revenue for different areas is also an excellent way to analyze a physician's practice for the benefit of our own business. We should know how to prepare a balance sheet, a cash flow statement, and an income statement per year, which will help to improve the management of a small company such as a doctor's practice.

Suggested Reading

1. John A. Tracy. *How to Read a Financial Report*. New York, NY: Wiley, 2003.
2. Richard E. McDermott and Kevin D. Stocks. *Code Blue*. Syracuse, UT: Traemus, 2002.
3. Rhonda W. Sides and Michael A. Roberts. *Accounting Handbook for Medical Practice*. New York, NY: Wiley, 2000.
4. Ryears Ended June 30, 2015, and 2016 – Saonm.org. https://www.saonm.org/media/audits/962-A_Western_New_Mexico_University_Foundation.
5. Is it Relevant to Switch to Structured Framemaker. *Adobe Forums*. Available at: https://forums.adobe.com/thread/1184657.

Chapter 9

Stark Law and Its Impact on Physicians

Centers For Medicare & Medicaid Services (CMS) Definition

Section 1877 of the Social Security Act (the Act) (42 U.S.C. 1395nn) is also known as the physician self-referral law and commonly referred to as "Stark Law."[1]

Stark Law was created to limit self-referral and has expanded to restrict physicians and hospital practice. Physicians cannot ask each other what their fee is; we cannot ask what salary our colleagues receive or about the contract of another physician in our or another specialty. This is all against Stark Law.

But in the United States (US), the free market and competition require many businesses to check their competitor prices and adjust accordingly. In this way, the healthcare system and hospitals can bring costs to the lowest level.

- Avoid physicians making referrals for specific designated health services (DHS) payable by Medicare to an entity with which the physician (or an immediate family member) has a financial relationship (ownership, investment, or compensation), unless an exception applies.
- Avoid claims to Medicare by billing another individual, object, or third party payer, for those specific services.
- .Individualize and create regulatory limitations for financial relationships that do not pose a risk of program or patient abuse.

Stark Law is contrary to the union of physicians. Hospitals do not like unions, and they will fight against them to the end. Unions, despite their pitfalls, could become a way for physicians to obtain accurate reimbursement and recognition. Maybe the old saying "unify we are stronger" is true, even if most of my senior colleagues are afraid and offended by this concept. But what can physicians now do to protect themselves? Not even our medical society has any power…!

Stark Law is achieving the goal of keeping physicians isolated and defenseless. It might have been a good idea 20 years ago, but now, with healthcare controlled by corporations, the physician is at the mercy of the corporation and is very vulnerable.

What Do You Need to Know about Stark Law?

Stark Law focuses primarily on the following health services:

- Laboratory services
- Physical therapy services
- Occupational therapy services
- Outpatient speech–language pathology services
- Radiology and other specific imaging services
- Radiation therapy services and supplies
- Durable medical equipment and supplies
- Parenteral and enteral nutrients, equipment, and supplies
- Prosthetics, orthotics, and prosthetic devices and supplies
- Home health services
- Outpatient prescription drugs
- Inpatient and outpatient hospital services

Ayala Ellison[2] wrote an excellent article summarizing the most critical points of Stark Law. Stark, acting 20 years ago, started to limit physician self-referral. Unfortunately, Stark Law has become a significant set of regulations with the goal of regulating the fee-for-service system.

Here are the eight things to know about Stark Law according to Ayala Ellison's article:

1. In 1989, Congress passed the Ethics in Patient Referrals Act, which was dubbed Stark I after Rep. Pete Stark, a Democrat from California, who sponsored the initial bill.
2. The original statute was quite simple. It sought to ban physician self-referral for designated services when Medicare or another government payer covered a patient. Self-referral occurs when physicians refer patients for selected health services to hospitals,
3. The goal was to eliminate any financial motivation for physicians to send patients for unnecessary testing that could raise overall healthcare costs.

4. The original ordinance was expanded in January 1995, when Stark II went into effect. Over the next decade, CMS published a series of regulations implementing the physician self-referral law. Today, there is a sprawling group of rules and statutes collectively named Stark Law.

5. Stark Law has numerous exceptions, each of which carries its detailed requirements. Many of the limitations on compensation to a physician do not take into account the value or volume of a physician's referrals or other business generated between the parties, including payment at fair market value.

6. Violating the Stark means that all Medicare funds paid under the improper arrangement must be repaid, which could total tens of millions of dollars. The organization could face Medicare exclusion and False Claims Act liability as well.

7. Any payment submitted to the government which violates Stark Law is considered false or fraudulent. This is liability under the False Claims Act, according to the American Bar Association. Whistle-blowers under the *qui tam* provision of the False Claims Act are included.

8. Whistle-blowers have an incentive since they are entitled to up to 30% of the government's recovery in False Claims Act cases. The penalties authorized under the False Claims Act were raised in 2016 to a range of $10,781–$21,563 per claim.

Complexity is Overwhelming

The complexity of Stark Law has left hospital executives, Congress, and CMS struggling with the boundaries of the legislation — especially as the healthcare industry replaces traditional fee-for-service medicine with value-based care. Stark Law requires that physicians receive only fair market prices for their services, and there are severe costs associated with technical violations.

Common technical breaches of Stark Law include lack of documentation to support fair market value, failure to accurately describe services rendered, and an inability to change the terms of writing when compensation or duties change. Reports are made on the effects of Stark Law and the Anti-Kickback Statute on the industry's transition to value-based payment models. The Department of Health and Human Services (HHS) reported that some gainsharing and similar arrangements could be structured in a way that does not violate the Anti-Kickback Statute and meets the requirements of Stark Law. However, HHS noted the current fraud and abuse laws may serve as an impediment to robust, innovative programs that align providers by using financial incentives to achieve quality standards, generate cost savings and reduce waste.

Legislators and hospital leaders have expressed concerns about Stark Law in recent years. For instance, during a Senate Finance Committee hearing, Chairman Orrin Hatch (R-Utah) said Stark Law has become too complicated, creating obstacles in the transition from the antiquated fee-for-service model.

Sen. Hatch's views were echoed by several healthcare leaders during the hearing, including Ronald Paulus, MD, CEO of Asheville, N.C.-based Mission Health. Dr. Paulus said that problems with the physician self-referral law couldn't be fixed by tinkering around the edges. He believes a full repeal is necessary to allow health systems to move forward with population health efforts.

Anti-Kickback

It is very difficult to define the differences between the Stark statute and the Anti-Kickback Statute. Not only are they not the same law, but they also have a very different scope and are in two different sections of the Social Security Act.[3]

- The Stark statute pertains only to physician referrals under Medicare and Medicaid ("physicians" includes chiropractors and dentists but not midlevel providers, such as nurse practitioners and physician assistants).
- The Anti-Kickback Statute is far broader and affects anyone engaging in business with a federal healthcare program.[4]
- The Stark statute does not require harmful intent (i.e., a tainted financial relationship violates Stark Law, regardless of good intentions); the Anti-Kickback Statute involves purpose, but it must have a specific intent (i.e., not just plan that might merely be inferred from a pattern of behavior).
- The Stark statute exceptions define the boundaries of permissible behavior. The statute is a prohibition that can only be overcome by complying explicitly with an exception. The anti-kickback "safe harbor" regulations describe transactions that may tend to induce referrals but don't necessarily violate the law. The safe harbor regulations state clearly that transactions that don't meet a safe harbor don't necessarily break the statute; a prosecutor will evaluate the facts and circumstances to make that determination.[3]
- A Stark violation is punishable by civil money penalties; an anti-kickback violation is punishable by exclusion from federal healthcare programs, criminal penalties of up to $25,000 in fines, or up to 5 years in jail (or both) and a $50,000 civil money penalty for each violation.

In every situation where the Stark statute applies, the anti-kickback statute applies too.

Access to Law: The Legal Environment

Rules set by the Social Security Act[5] had the same requirements:

1. The lease is set out in writing, signed by the parties, and specifies the premises covered by the contract.

2. The space rented or leased does not exceed that which is reasonable and necessary for the legitimate business purposes.
3. Lease or rental and is used exclusively by the lessee.[6]
4. The contract provides for a term of rental or rent for at least one year with remuneration from an entity under an arrangement.
5. The agreement is set out in writing, signed by the parties, and specifies the services covered by the settlement.[1]

Reasonable Arrangements

1. The deal includes all of the services to be provided by the physician (or an immediate family member of such physician) to the entity.[7]
2. The aggregate functions contracted for do not exceed those that are reasonable and necessary for the legitimate business purposes of the arrangement.[8]
3. The term of the agreement is for one year.[9]
4. The compensation to be paid over the duration of the deal is set in advance, does not exceed the fair market value, and is not determined in a manner that takes into account the volume or usefulness of any referrals or other business generated between the parties.[10]
5. Services to be performed under the arrangement do not involve counseling or promotion or a business arrangement or other activity that violates any State or Federal law.[5]
6. The method meets such other requirements as the Secretary may impose by regulation as needed to protect against program or patient abuse.[11]

Physician Incentive Plan Exception

In the case of a physician incentive plan (as defined in clause (ii)) between a physician and an entity, the compensation may be determined in a manner (through a withhold, capitation, bonus, or otherwise), that takes into account directly or indirectly the volume or value of any referrals or other business generated.[1]

Employee Physician

A physician is considered to be "employed by" or an "employee" of an entity under the usual common law rules applicable in determining the employer-employee relationship (as applied for purposes of section 3121(d)(2) of the Internal Revenue Code of 1986).[11]

Fair Market Value

The term "fair market value" is consistent with the general market value concerning rentals or leases. The cost of rental property for general commercial purposes (not taking into account its intended use) and, in the case of a contract of space, not adjusted to reflect the additional value the prospective lessee or lessor would attribute to the proximity or convenience to the lessor where the lessor is a potential source of patient referrals to the lessee.[1]

Group Practice

The term "group practice" means a group of two or more physicians legally organized as a partnership, professional corporation, foundation, not-for-profit corporation, faculty practice plan, or similar association.

The physician who is a member of the group provides the full range of services which a physician routinely provides, including medical care, consultation, diagnosis, or treatment, through the joint use of shared office space, facilities, equipment, and personnel.[5]

Notes

1. Physician Self-Referral. *Centers for Medicare and Medicaid Services.* Available at: https://www.cms.gov/medicare/fraud-and-abuse/physicianselfreferral/index.html.
2. Ayla Ellison. 2017, February 18. 15 Things to Know About Stark Law. *Becker's Hospital Review.* Available at: https://www.beckershospitalreview.com/legal-regulatory-issues/15-things-to-know-about-stark-law-021717.html.
3. Alice G. Gosfield. The Stark Truth About the Stark Law: Part I. *Fam Pract Manag*, 10(10): 27–33, 2003.
4. Grants, Clinical Trials, and Contracts. *LSU Health New Orleans.* Available at: https://www.medschool.lsuhsc.edu/fiscal_affairs/docs/GeneralFinancial/Grants ContractsTrials.pdf.
5. Limitation on Certain Physician Referrals. *Social Security Administration.* Available at: https://www.ssa.gov/OP_Home/ssact/title18/1877.htm.
6. 411.356 42 CFR Ch. Iv (10–1–03 Edition). *Centers for Medicare and Medicaid Services.* Available at: https://www.cms.gov/Medicare/Medicare-Fee-for-Service-Payment/ClinicalLabFeeSched/Downloads/411_357.pdf.
7. Title 42: The Public Health and Welfare. *Government Publishing Office.* Available at: https://www.gpo.gov/fdsys/pkg/USCODE-2015-title42/pdf/USCODE-2015-title42-chap7-subchapXVIII-partE-sec1395nn.pdf.
8. Electronic Code of Federal Regulations. *AAPC.* Available at: https://www.aapc.com/training/documents/cpco/electronic-code-of-federal-regulation.
9. Victoria Heller Johnson. 2009. The Kosenske Case and Stark: An Important Lesson for Physician-Hospital Arrangements. *Fox Rothschild.* Available at: https://www.foxrothschild.com/publications/the-kosenske-case-and-stark-an-important-lesson-for-physician-hospital-arrangements/.

10. Federal Stark Law (Patient Self-Referral): 1395nn. *American College of Physicians.* Available at: https://www.acponline.org/about-acp/chapters-regions/united-states/florida-chapter/federal-stark-law-patient-self-referral-1395nn.
11. Limitation on Certain Physician Referrals. *Legal Information Institute.* Available at: https://www.law.cornell.edu/uscode/text/42/1395nn.

Chapter 10

Healthcare Grade Website Interferences on Clinical Practice

Uncontrolled Voices on the Web

In this day and age, physicians are judged by quality measures. There are metrics for physicians in every specialty. Every healthcare provider performs some action that gets reported. These measures are essential, and most of them are objective. However, there are also evaluations from patients that are much more subjective and can significantly impact a physician's market and referral bases.

Similar to how people review restaurants, patients can evaluate their physicians. Unlike restaurants, however, these evaluations are mostly negative. My observation has been that, in medicine, when the patient is satisfied, he or she very rarely reports this after being discharged. He or she might make a report right after the visit or at the end of treatment. Patients that go home dissatisfied are usually the ones that go to the webpage and write a negative review to ensure others know about their poor experience. The same also happens when patients talk about hospitals. While this feedback is not a real reflection of the physician, it becomes difficult to defend physicians in hospitals from mostly negative posted comments.

The problem arises not from the negative comments themselves, but from a lack of examination of the comments. Websites that provide a review service will group any and all comments on the physician that saw the patient. Therefore, if a patient complains about the waiting time, the cold coffee, the attitude of a nurse, etc., all of those comments are graded and grouped under the physician. The corporations associated with the websites will project the negative score or comments first, so it's easier for patients to find. The caveat of all of this is that insurance companies will use these quality reports to cut down on reimbursement for the hospital and physician.

These complaints that are unrelated to the healthcare service provided by the physician are nevertheless connected to the physician. Furthermore, hospitals will use these quality reports to judge their physicians. Very few articles are written on this critical issue, which is affecting everybody in healthcare, physicians, nurses, and hospitals. Nurses association have tried to do something about it but are in the early stages.

Hospitals will also use web comments to create sham peer reviews on physicians.

Adverse Effects of the Web

This problem is affecting all healthcare services and providers. I agree with the concerns voiced by nurse Mary Guy Bucnis in a recent article:

> The entire health field is changing drastically and in a terrible way. Hospitals are being rated with surveys like that of hotels. They are reimbursed for patient satisfaction. Now I want all of my patients to have the best stay possible; however, realistically the hospital is a place for you to heal. You would rather pick a hospital based on the risk of infection or what is known as sentinel events (deadly accidents or mistakes) over how well they kissed your butt. Let's be real. We want to stay alive in the hospital and stay safe. We live in a world where we expect to have everyone cater to our every little need (Bucnis, 2014).[1]

This is an article published in 2014. The fact that this article was written 4 years ago indicates that these quality reports are affecting everybody in the wrong manner.

I examined one website, *reputation.com*, because of how nicely its timeframe and numbers match up. Other websites, or even a simple Google search, will show a similar trend of presenting the negative comments first and proudly. The absurdness is that these comments are overwhelmingly skewed toward negative experiences, resulting in unjustified negative reputations for physicians.

Thousands of Self-Reporting Web Sites

There is an increasing number of evaluation sites included and reviewed by *reputation.com*, and this number is growing every year (see Table 10.1).

The ratings on these sites range from 0 to 1,000. To make it easier for the consumer to read, *reputation.com* dramatically diminishes the range to a 1–5 scale

Table 10.1   Web Pages Where You Can Evaluate Physicians

	Rate 1–5 (Negative–Positive)
Review all time	
Rating all time	
Reviews this month rating	
Citysearch	
Facebook	
Google-local	
Health Grades	
Insider pages	
Kudzu	
MerchantCircle	
RateMDs	
Superpages	
UCompare Health Care	
Vitals	
Yahoo! Local	
Yellow Pages	
Yelp	
ZocDoc	

(where one is the lowest and five is excellent). *Reputation.com* sorts the reviews so that the negative reports appear on the first page, boldly highlighting negative comments in red, with better reviews further down the page, boldly highlighting positive remarks in green (a color that can also be harder to distinguish on a computer screen).

My Research

To better understand the depth of the problem, I performed a review of my cases and reports. I reviewed cases I performed in the operating room and the endoscopic suite over a 5-year period for which I can provide accurate numbers. I also considered the patients I saw in the office who did not get any surgery. I located all negative comments to understand what went wrong or what the problem was.

Let's Look at Numbers

Because this search intended to look at reviews posted to a ratings website, a single percentage will suffice for statistical analysis. No other factors are examined.

In the 5-year period, I had six negative comments and six positive comments posted to my page on *reputation.com*. My average score was 3.3 in 2014. One negative feedback in the last year brought my grade for 2014 below a 2.5 rating.

Within the same 5-year period, my case log in the operating room and the GI labs showed 4898 cases (or patients seen). Office visits for patients that did not undergo surgery and came for post-surgery follow-ups amount to an additional 2754 patients (7652 patients in total).

Excluding the patients seen for post-surgery follow-ups, only 0.122% of patients expressed a complaint about the services they received. Including the total amount of patients, the percentage drops to 0.078%.

Upon further examination of the content of the negative comments, I found that:

- Two patients were not satisfied with their surgery due to pre-explained, common, post-operation side effects.
- Two patients were not satisfied due to issues with the hospital or office staff.
- One comment was from a patient who was turned down for surgery,
- One comment was by a family member who was upset that I ordered too many tests for their father before the actual operation.

A look at only the negative comments that were based on medical issues (two in 5 years out of 4898 cases) yields a percentage of 0.040% (or 0.001% for total cases).

Let's Do the Statistics

From the statistics, only 0.001%–0.040% of patients had a negative experience. Alternatively, this means that 99.96%–99.99% of the remaining patients had no complaints or just did not feel the need to rate. It is worth noting that the positive data are not readily presented to the general population on websites like *reputation. com*. This includes referring physicians who may want to transfer their patient to a surgeon or people working for insurance companies who wish to incorporate reputable physicians into their networks. The only information readily available is six negative comments and six positive comments. There is also no mention of how many *other* patients I have seen.

Nobody Reads Comments

The first thing we understand that nobody reads the report. Most people count the report only. Which, by itself, is not right. Let's look at the comments. Two comments describe the complaints of patients following their surgery. They complained about some pain in the area where the operation occurred. As a physician, I am obligated to discuss everything about an operation: what prerequisites are necessary to meet before the surgery, what will happen during the operation, and what will occur as a result of the surgery. Primarily, the patients, in these cases, knew that there could be some pain following the surgery, given how invasive it was.

One other patient wrote a negative comment because his clearance for surgery was denied by his cardiologist. He had multiple medical problems, and his heart was not in a condition that could withstand surgery. Due to this denial, he wrote a negative comment.

The next three comments help illustrate the absurdness of these review websites.

There were two comments that described dissatisfaction with issues at the hospital. I found that one patient was upset with his or her nursing care, while another was upset with the medical assistant in the office. Unfortunately, the internet review sites do not have subsections where specific complaints can be listed. Instead, the rating websites have these comments that register as physician-related comments. In other words, no matter who may have been in involved in the healthcare service, the problem is attributed to the physician!

The last comment has a story to it that supports the observation that there is no further examination of quality reports. It was a comment from an individual whom I had never interacted with face-to-face. Instead, I had communicated with her father. Her father was admitted to hospital for dehydration, high alcohol levels, cirrhosis, angina, possible kidney failure, and (after examining the patient) a left inguinal hernia. He had lived with this hernia for at least 10 years but saw a doctor for it at the Veteran Hospital. A hernia alone validates surgery. However, due to his other medical issues, it was paramount to discuss the operation as an elective surgery that had gained medical clearance.

His admission was in October. No family members came to visit him during this time. He did not come to my office then. Instead, he came to my office in March (5 months later!). Again, no family present. After a discussion with the patient, the surgery was scheduled for a couple of weeks later. On the day of the operation, he did not show up.

He returned to my office at the end of April and we re-started the process once more. A new surgery date was chosen in May. Once again, no family accompanied him on the consultation day or the day of the surgery. Right before the surgery, he told me he did not want to do it for the following reasons:

1. Nobody was with him, and he planned to walk back home afterward.
2. He wanted to leave for a fishing trip in 2 days.

3. He had had an episode of bleeding the day before but did not report it to anybody. Given the circumstances, I called his GI doctor and canceled the surgery.

Soon after, I found a disparaging comment on the web written by the daughter of this patient (whom I did not see even once during the 7 months) stating that it was wrong of me that I waited to perform her father's surgery. To her defense, she probably did not understand her father's medical condition or his multiple missed appointments. However, it is precisely these unclear circumstances in her negative comment that allow other patients, hospitals, and insurance companies to say I am whatever they want to say I am. This, unfortunately, is the danger of web pages open to all. You can say everything you want, and there is no discussion!

Protecting Us From the Web

Physicians are at the mercy of these quality reporting websites, unlike other things that are subject to review. For example, restaurants can still be successful if their comments are "the room was too cold" or "there was no sign for the restroom." Teachers also face something similar. They receive negative comments about how difficult a class was for a student who did not do well in the class, despite also having multiple, successful students who say the opposite. Even presidential elections will garner negative comments that are more severe and dramatic, although a president only needs the majority of the country to vote for him or her. So, even if there are negative comments, a restaurant, a teacher, or even a president can still thrive, but a physician cannot.

So, the question becomes: Why do physicians suffer so much from comments that do not directly describe the healthcare service they provided? Why should physicians be penalized for a lack of responsibility on the part of patients for their obligations? Should the satisfaction or dissatisfaction of relatives who were not involved in the care of their loved ones count in the evaluation of physicians?

Smack Eating

This is a smack, a deep smack. My argument is that these evaluation websites do not provide an encompassing review of a physician, and therefore negatively impact their market and career.

I chose to pursue a surgical career because it is my passion. I want to help and serve others. Sadly, it becomes increasingly difficult to work if only a mere six negative comments determine my capability as a surgeon. It is my shared hope with other physicians that patients, administrators, hospitals, and insurance companies will look past the numbers; however, nobody will stand on the front line of this ongoing problem to help fight for physicians.

The evaluation data provided by patient-driven, physician-evaluation websites are starting to smack us in the face. It makes for lousy marketing: A smack-eating!

Note

1. Mary Guy Bucnis. 2014, November 19. The Dirty Secret That Is Destroying Nurses. *Mighty Nurse*, Shift Wise Inc. Available at: www.mightynurse.com/the-dirty-secret-that-is-ruining-nursing-stories/#sthash.kxBWRM4s.dpufI.

Suggested Reading

1. Tauriq Moosa. 2014, September 12. Comment Sections are Poison: Handle with Care. *Guardian*. Available at: https://www.theguardian.com/science/brain-flapping/2014/sep/12/comment-sections-toxic-moderation.
2. Mary Stockley. 2016, May 26. Why You Can't Trust Things You Copy and Paste From Web Pages. *Naked Security*. Available at: https://nakedsecurity.sophos.com/2016/05/26/why-you-cant-trust-things-you-cut-and-paste-from-web-pages/.
3. https://chrome.google.com/webstore/detail/wot-web-of-trust-website/bhmmomiinigofkjcapegjjndpbikblnp?hl=en.
4. Neil Patel. 50 Reasons Your Website Deserves to be Penalized by Google. Available at: https://blog.kissmetrics.com/penalized-by-google/.

Chapter 11

Healthcare Impact on Physicians: Not Healthy!

Burnout

Burnout is a significant problem in the United States and is reaching 70% among physicians. Burnout is characterized as a person who is emotional, exhausted, and fatigued and, if you like, feels the loss of a sense of personal accomplishment. This has significant repercussions for both individual providers and the healthcare organization.

Burnout is one cause of a decrease in quality care and patient satisfaction, but also affects the private life of the physician and can end in drug addiction and increase suicide rates. On the medical side, it can increase medical errors and the risk of malpractice.

The physician is caring for people, but there is nothing set in healthcare to ensure that the physician is cared for.

Most physicians have reported that the cause of burnout is secondary to work overload, insufficient rewards, unfair treatment by the hospital, and a breakdown in communication between the physician and the healthcare administrator. There are a lot of conflicts in values between healthcare facilities and physicians, with a push to produce more and the risk of decreasing the quality. The physician is overwhelmed by bureaucratic tasks that take away from valuable patient care time; this also comes with an increase in medical malpractice risk. Physicians are also concerned that they do not have enough time for continuous medical education because they are spending more time documenting electronic medical records. This latter system is built by non-physicians for the use of physicians and, of course, does not match clinical practice; therefore, the documentation is lengthy and elaborate and does not get to the point that flows.

The physician is not part of medical decisions and strategic choices in the hospital and does not participate in crucial meetings to discuss new algorithms for treating patients, and therefore can get frustrated.

Physicians feel that they are the "second victims" of an organization. For example, when somebody in the department goes down, everybody goes down. This has happened to me.

The president went to jail, my boss killed himself, and everybody that was hired by the organization became second victims and were pushed out of the hospital. That should never happen to anybody after my experience. Physicians lost the control of their medical practices, and they felt that they were not rewarded. There is a sense of unfairness regarding doing more work for less, and physicians perceive a conflict between the profit motive and the quality of care.

Most organizations hire physicians based on a 40-hour week, but the physician works double those hours. Therefore, the hourly rate for the physician becomes more similar to that for nurses. There is no recognition of extra hours.

It is interesting that burnout is recognized in many companies and in industries, but not in healthcare.

It is also very difficult for a physician to admit to burnout, and to depression or other issues, because, if you talk to somebody, it will be reported to the board and the physician can have his or her license restricted or suspended. Therefore, physicians are afraid of repercussion.

Rewards

One thing that would probably solve some of these problems is to increase the respect given to the physician for the extra hours worked, for the quality of his or her work, and for the service to the community. Monetary and public awards need to be in place to reward hard-working physicians in clinical practice.

Mark Twain said, "I can live for two months on a good compliment."

More than a century later, this is still true—any organizational change initiative brings uncertainty, but when change is successful, it is essential to recognize the effort of the team and the individuals involved, and reward them.

Thank the person, and shake his or her hand. Make it both public and private, and do not just send an email, letter, or note. Match the achievement with appropriate recognition for the physician, set more goals that the person can achieve in a way they became much more involved and even a better person. Most crucial of all is timeliness; don't wait a month before thanking people for their achievements.

Moral Injury

Talbot and Dean[1] reported in a recent article about physicians and moral injury, reporting exactly the symptoms of burning out of a moral distress secondary to the lack of recognition of our role and importance in the hospital. We lost all! We are becoming secretary of the medical floor of the surgical floor, we are treated as robot and housekeeper and we still keep all the responsibilities. From their article: "The moral injury of health care is not the offense of killing another human in the context of war. It is being unable to provide high-quality care and healing in the context of health care."

We feel useless. But nobody understands that if one day all the administrative personnel live the hospital, the hospital will still function, but if all the physician leave there is no longer a hospital.

We have the power of being the healthcare provider but we do not use it and we become a little more depressed every day.

Malpractice

Patients do not understand science, but they do recognize good manners. They look at your office and observe whether it is clean, and whether you look professional and have friendly, adept staff. If they have to wait too long for appointments, how long it will take to make the next meeting, etc.[2]

Doctors who make a positive impression on the patient:

1. Appear unrushed
2. Show interest in the patient as a person
3. Speak in a friendly and uncondescending tone
4. Tend to rarely be sued
   - First claim by the time the physician is 45 years old
     • Highest-risk specialties: 88%
     • Lowest- risk specialties: 36%
   - Claim by the time the physician is 65 years old
     • Highest-risk specialties: 99%
     • Lowest-risk specialties: 75%
   - More than 95% of physicians react to being sued by experiencing periods of emotional distress during all or some portions of the lengthy process.
   - Feelings of intense anger, frustration, inner tension, and insomnia are frequent throughout this period.
   - Most malpractice cases are settled or dismissed.
   - About 2% of claims are tried.
   - Physicians win about 75% of the time.
   - Payments above policy limits rarely, if ever, come from a physician's assets, especially when physicians have policy limits greater than or equal to $500,000

Side Effects on Physicians

- Anger
- Denial
- Guilt/shame
- Feelings of betrayal
- Loss of self-esteem
- Isolation
- Physical illness
- Substance abuse
- Depression/suicide risk
- Risk of ethical violations

The physician will be personally angry; he or she will feel disillusioned, and may have a global mistrust of patients.

He or she starts to magnify his or her self-doubt and questions his or competence.

The physician feels down, depressed and cynical, isolated, frustrated, and unjustly singled out

He or she starts thinking about changing practice, leaving medicine, suicide, being intolerant toward patients.

He or she starts changing his or her relationships and attitudes toward friends and family.

What Are the Measures to Protect Against Lawsuits?

- Documentation
- Strategy in patient regimens
- The right nurse–receptionist relationship
- Proactivity: sending a letter, making phone calls for follow-up, etc.

Communicate effectively with your patients. Try to make them understand why they are there, the goals for their care and treatment, and the possible outcomes.

Treat the patient as a friend, not as a lower class of citizen. Even if you think patients will not understand the science, try to create a scenario that they can understand and that avoids any impression of talking down to them.

- To help ensure proper follow-up, one excellent strategy to implement in your patient regimen is a discussion period with the patient before he or she leaves the office or hospital following surgery.
- It is essential to record this follow-up in writing, sending one copy home with the patient and placing a second copy into his or her chart, with documentation that a follow-up discussion was had with the patient.

- Doctors also need to encourage patients to schedule the next appointment before they leave the office. This is easily accomplished if the office is set up with an electronic system; follow-up phone calls are much more difficult in an office that is not computerized.
- Nurses and receptionists are an integral part of your team. As they become more involved in patient care, they play an increasingly vital role in ensuring comprehensive follow-up.
- The best defense against an attorney who plans to sue you for negligence in following-up with a patient is to demonstrate that there has been quality communication and proper documentation of the fact that all efforts were made to complete follow-up for the patient.
- Your attorney can thus argue that the patient understood the recommendation but failed to follow the surgeon's advice.
- Unfortunately, if this is not documented in the progress notes, this argument cannot be made in your defense.
- Many juries assume that the surgeon has superior knowledge and that he or she should take steps to ensure patient compliance, even though this is not a simple task to accomplish.
- While most agree that patients must take responsibility for their own healthcare, some juries think that the doctor alone must make sure that the patient complies with follow-up.
- Juries reach this conclusion without taking into consideration how much work this involves, how many patients the physician has, and how limited the personnel are.

Suicide Factors and Rate

There are multiple stress factors affecting physicians:

- Frustration
- Inner tension
- Difficulty concentrating
- Insomnia
- Family and social withdrawal
- Irritability
- Loss of interest
- Fatigue
- Decreased sex drive
- GI symptoms
- Suicidal ideation

The inability to cope successfully may lead to maladaptive behavioral patterns such as:

- Aloofness
- Irritability
- Disruptive behaviors
- Increased use of alcohol or drugs
- Increased risk of unethical behavior

Physicians, in general, have a higher rate of suicide than other professional groups and the public. Female physicians' suicide rates are reported to be up to 400% higher than for women in other professions. Male physicians' rates are 50%–70% higher.[3]

Suicide:

- Seventh leading cause of death in US men
- Fifth leading cause of death in US women
- Third leading cause of death in US individual aged 15–24
- Most prevalent in the elderly and in adolescents
- Highest rate: men over 85
- Physician health experts say that as many as 400 US physicians take their lives each year
- Major depressive disorder (MDD) affects 13%–17% of Americans every year
- The rate of MDD in physicians is similar to that in the general population: 13% of male physicians and 20% of female physicians
- One-third of medical residents have a diagnosis of MDD during residency
- 30% of physicians show MDD one year after graduation
- MDD is a risk factor for suicide
- Physicians who make suicide attempts are much more likely to complete suicide than non-physicians
- The rate of suicide in male physicians is 70% higher, and the rate in female physicians is 250%–400% higher than in the general population

The Suicide Crisis

Demands on physicians have changed, and navigating healthcare has become more complex and challenging. Proper action needs to be taken to protect wellness among physicians and trainees.

Major organizations have not yet made policy changes, despite the evident crises that pose a 300 rate decrease of suicide in the physician. "One million Americans lose their doctors to suicide each year."

In the past 3 years, more than 40% of fellow physicians and residents have faced symptoms of anxiety or depression. Residents have felt isolated, without any way to seek mental health resources. Many physicians fear the negative consequences and stigma surrounding the admission of a mental health diagnosis.[4]

On the resident ACGME website, there is an entire page dedicated to the topic, but despite adequate information regarding physician suicide and physician wellness, there are no resources that can be translated into the everyday lives of physicians, especially for trainees.[2]

"Nine of 10 doctors discourage others from joining the profession, and 300 physicians commit suicide every year," writes internist, Dr. Daniela Drake. "High doctor suicide rates have been reported since 1858," family physician, Dr. Pamela Wible, points out. Suicide is the "second-leading cause of death for residents—and the leading cause for male residents," states Dr. Nathaniel P. Morris, resident physician in psychiatry at Stanford University School of Medicine.[2]

Notes

1. Simon G. Talbot. 2018, July 28. Physicians Aren't "Burning Out." They're Suffering From Moral Injury. *Statnews*. Available at: https://www.statnews.com/2018/07/26/physicians-not-burning-out-they-are-suffering-moral-injury/.
2. Cherilyn Cecchini. 2018, February 22. A Stigma No Physician Can Afford. *Bag of Pediatricks*. Available at: http://bagofpediatricks.com/2018/02/22/a-stigma-no-physician-can-afford/.
3. Elizabeth Lee Vliet. Physician Suicide Rates Have Climbed Since Obamacare Passed. *Physicians News Digest*. Available at: https://physiciansnews.com/2015/05/19/physician-suicide-rates-have-climbed-since-obamacare-passed/.
4. Student Opportunities | College of Behavioral, Social, and Health Sciences. Available at: https://www.clemson.edu/cbshs/departments/political-science/students/index.html.

Suggested Reading

1. Dike Drummond. Physician Burnout: Its Origin, Symptoms, and Five Main Causes. *Fam Prract Manag*, 22(5): 42–47, 2015.
2. Joanne Finnegan. 2017, May 30. The Top 5 Reasons for Malpractice Lawsuits Against Doctors. *Fierce Healthcare*. Available at: https://www.fiercehealthcare.com/practices/top-five-reasons-for-malpractice-lawsuits-against-docs.
3. Carol Peckham. 2018, January 17. Medscape National Physician Burnout & Depression Report 2018. *Medscape*. Available at: https://www.medscape.com/slideshow/2018-lifestyle-burnout-depression-6009235.

BROKEN SYSTEM

Chapter 12

Health Insurance: Maximum Reimbursement, at What Cost?

Decreasing Reimbursement

Reimbursement for healthcare has been under downward pressure for several years. Newspapers have published articles citing the "greed" of hospitals, physicians, and other healthcare providers.[1] Congress has reacted by instructing Medicare to control payments to keep the Medicare trust fund "budget neutral." Consequently, the result has been decreased payments across the healthcare system to both hospitals and providers. Although there is ample research available, it seems that virtually no one in Washington, D.C., wants to tackle the causes of the healthcare crisis. The primary intention of the Affordable Care Act (ACA) was to control and lower healthcare costs by spreading the risk among both the healthy and the unhealthy populations. It was also intended to provide ongoing relationships with primary care physicians (PCPs) to avoid the overuse of emergency departments and to allow patients to seek treatment without delay. By focusing on good health, ongoing relationships with the medical community, and prompt treatment, the hope and intent of the ACA was to decrease the overall cost of healthcare for the entire country. Unfortunately, it did not address many of the causes of increased healthcare costs over the past 30 years. This chapter will highlight several significant factors responsible for the rapid rise in health-related expenditures.

Accountable care organizations (ACOs) are structured to be the equivalent of "one-stop shopping," where all of the patient's needs are obtained through a single healthcare system for diagnostics, treatment, and rehabilitation.

Managing Healthcare Costs

Controlling healthcare costs is not easy; we need to change the culture with a fresh perspective on the way to keep employees engaged in this pursuit.

The latest insights on evolving tools available to engage employees in bringing healthcare spending under control can be found in the article "New Cures For Health Costs."[2] This article describes:

1. How savings come from adopting a holistic approach
2. Leaning on high-tech for high return on investment
3. How reducing spending requires increasing engagement

Developing trust and investing in follow-up and follow-through are a few of the key insights shared. Applying these fresh approaches can improve the health of your workforce as a critical element of your business strategy.

Value-Based Programs

The Hospital Value-Based Program (VBP) is outlined in Section 1886(o) of the Social Security Act. The Hospital VBP is the nation's first national pay-for-performance program for acute care hospitals and serves as an essential driver in redesigning how the Centers for Medicare & Medicaid Services (CMS) pay for care and services based on the quality and value of care, and not just the quantity.

Purpose of the Baseline Measures Report

The Hospital VBP Baseline Measures Report allows providers to monitor their performance in all domains and measures required for the Hospital VBP Program.

The hospital's Baseline Measures Report includes the following sections:

1. The Clinical Care Detail Report provides details on the four Clinical Care measures, including the number of eligible discharges and the baseline period rate. The achievement threshold and benchmark for each Clinical Care measure are also displayed.
2. The Person and Community Engagement Detail Report provide details on the eight HCAHPS dimensions, including baseline period rates, floor values, achievement thresholds, and benchmarks. The number of completed surveys is also displayed. HCAHPS (also known as Hospital CAHPS) stands for Hospital Consumer Assessment of Healthcare Providers and Systems.

3. The Safety Measures Detail Report provides details on the Agency for Healthcare Research and Quality (AHRQ) Patient Safety Indicator composite measure (PSI-90), the PC-01 measure, and the following healthcare associated infection (HAI) measures:
   - AHRQ PSI-90 composite measures
   - Healthcare-associated infections
   - Process measures
   - Efficiency and cost reduction detail report
   - Clinical care measures in hospitals

President and CEO of the Center for Healthcare Quality and Payment Reform, Harold D. Miller reported: "The goals of value-based payment are to give healthcare providers adequate resources to deliver efficient, quality care and to remove the penalties that exist today for improving quality and efficiency. Episode-of-care payment and comprehensive care payment systems can help providers prevent health problems; prevent the occurrence of acute episodes among individuals who have health conditions; avert poor outcomes during major severe incidents, such as infections, complications, and hospital readmissions; and reduce the costs of successful treatment. By using payment changes to help address these significant sources of waste and inefficiency, healthcare costs can be reduced significantly without impacting care that patients need."[3]

Hospitals are getting bonuses under pay-for-performance systems and for reducing infections, but this does not change the underlying payment system and its rewards for providing more services. Medicare's rules excluding hospital-acquired infections from the diagnosis-related group (DRG) formula do not prevent hospitals from getting paid for the complications resulting from those infections or from receiving outlier payments for those cases.[3]

In contrast, if a hospital or physician has no incentive to ensure quality, they do not have an incentive to improve.

Proposals for "shared savings" payments to providers require a focus on outcomes but do not change the underlying fee-for-service structure and fail to provide any up-front resources to implement new services.[4] In contrast, comprehensive care payments give physicians and other providers awareness and accountability to deliver high-quality, efficient care.

A comprehensive care payment system also avoids penalizing providers for treating sicker patients—one of the major problems with traditional capitation payment systems—because the amount of the global care payment is secondary to the number and severity of a patient's health conditions.[3]

Setting the right payment *amount* (i.e., the price) is as important as using the correct payment *method*.[3] The amount has to be right: if it is too low, physicians will be unable to deliver quality care. If it is too high, there is no incentive to seek out efficiencies.

Another goal is to avoid antitrust concerns and to facilitate consensus among local payers on payment changes.[3] However, Medicare needs to be able to participate in such regionally defined payment reforms to achieve accurate alignment of incentives.

The first step is to understand the healthcare terms, as described in Table 12.1.

Understanding the Terms

A discounted fee is one that insurers negotiate with doctors, hospitals, and other healthcare providers in their network. Consulting charges reduce costs for you and for the insurance company and are an essential reason why insurers create incentives to use in-network providers and why you pay more when you don't. Unlike providers outside the network, those who are in-network have agreed to accept the discounted fees as full payment for services rendered. Each insurer has its list of allowed charges.[6]

Some insurance policies set a maximum amount an insurer will pay per year. If the amount is exceeded, the patients are required to pay the difference. However, most individual plans don't set an annual maximum benefit.[7]

Services or supplies your health plan agrees to cover. Covered benefits and excluded services differ from plan to plan.

One safety net for expensive services such as hospitalization is a catastrophic plan, which is essential because its premium may be lower than that of traditional

Table 12.1 Costs, Charges, and Reimbursement

Term	Definition
Cost	To providers: by delivering healthcare services to patients To payers: by paying providers for services rendered To patients: out-of-pocket costs for healthcare services
Charges	What is asked by a provider for healthcare goods or services that appear on a medical bill (The challenge of understanding health care costs. http://journalofethics.ama-assn.org/2015/11/stas1-1511.html)
Reimbursement	A payment made by insurances to a provider for services (fee-for-service), for each day in the hospital (per diem), for each episode of hospitalization (e.g., diagnosis-related groups, or DRGs), or for each patient considered to be under their care (capitation) (*American Medical Association Journal of Ethics* (n.d.). Retrieved from http://journalofethics.ama-assn.org/2015/11/pdf/stas1-1511.pdf)

Source: Adapted from *Understanding Value-Based Healthcare.* The challenge of understanding health care costs. http://journalofethics.ama-assn.org/2015/11/stas1-1511.html[5]

insurance. Unfortunately, this brings high deductibles, which means that the program begins providing coverage only after you've paid a specified amount. Some programs require you to pay a deductible of $10,000 or more before coverage kicks in.

In 2014, health services within the ACA gave directions on the services offered such as:

> as outpatient surgery, emergency services, hospitalization, maternity and newborn care, mental health and substance abuse services (including behavioral treatment and prescription drugs), rehabilitative and habilitative services and devices, laboratory services, preventive and wellness services, chronic disease management, and pediatric services including oral and vision care. Each state, however, will have significant latitude in establishing these benefits. Under the ACA, all plans were required to phase out annual dollar spending limits for these services by 2014.[6]

Notes

1. Brian Hudson. 2018, January 8. Top Concerns CNOs Face in 2018. *Avant Healthcare*. Available at: https://avanthealthcare.com/blog/cno-roundtable/top-concerns-cnos-face-in-2018.stml.
2. David McCann. New Cures for Health Costs. *Accolade*. Available at: https://d10j0m-6hqftivr.cloudfront.net/New-Cures-for-Health-Costs-CFO-Magazine-May-2016.pdf.
3. Harold D. Miller. Value-Based Payments, Outcomes, and Costs. In Pierre L. Yong, S. Saunders, LeighAnne Olsen (Eds.). *The Healthcare Imperative: Lowering Costs and Improving Outcomes*. Washington, DC: National Academies Press.
4. Harold D. Miller. How to Fix the Medicare Shared Savings Program. *Centre for Healthcare Quality and Payment Reform*. 2008. Available at: http://www.chqpr.org/downloads/How_to_Fix_the_Medicare_Shared_Savings_Program.pdf.
5. Vineet Arora, Christopher Moriates, Neel Shah. The Challenge of Understanding Health Care Costs and Charges. *AMA Journal of Ethics*, 17(11): 1046–1052. 2015. Available at: https://journalofethics.ama-assn.org/article/challenge-understanding-health-care-costs-and-charges/2015-11.
6. U.S. News Staff. 2014, November 14. Health Insurance Definitions: What the Terms Mean. *U.S. News*. Available at: https://health.usnews.com/health-news/health-insurance/articles/2014/11/14/health-insurance-definitions-what-the-terms-mean.
7. Insurance Terms. Grant Smith. Available at: https://grantsmith.com/insurance-terms.html.

Chapter 13

Healthcare: Who Is in Charge? Impossible Victory

Who Are the Customers?

A lot of the time, times CEOs come from factories, from the laboratory as they were tech one time, but none of them understand the complex and diverse knowledge needed to take care of the patient. Patients are not cars—each one is different, and physicians always have to "play well in defense" since they never know how the patient will do after medication and surgery.

Everybody wants to standardize the appropriate care; so maybe we need to regulate hospital administration and its approach to the essential customers.

There are only two customers in the hospital:

1. Patients
2. Physicians

It is time that administration goes and learns how to set medical practice and what the difference is between an internal medicine practice and a surgical practice, not just by numbers but by placing the physician in the best way they can practice. Let them do the job and evaluate them on the job and not on the rumors or other little things that hospitals create that have nothing to do with patient care.

That will increase retention and decrease physician discontent that results in the physician leaving after realizing how dangerous and badly managed the facility where they work is. Physicians are not stupid!

If you want the physician to take care of difficult patients, expect claims in this day and age, but then read the claims and see what happened. Most administration staff just count the claims instead of evaluating them. Of course, how can they evaluate them if they do not have medical knowledge? Here comes our point: business and healthcare are two different things, and doctors have been excluded from any hospital decisions with detriment to the physician, and ultimately to the hospitals that lose the physicians. This is a simple concept but is difficult to understand.

It is essential that administration understands physician practice if they want to remain in charge. If they are not capable, they will need to hire a chief medical officer (CMO) to do the job for them.

The best scenario is a good administrator or a physician CEO.

Who Cares?

According to basic understanding, healthcare is the industry that looks after the health of people who need it.

With this definition, there will be no question that the only ones that can do this are physicians and healthcare providers, *in primis* nurses.

Unfortunately, the primary job in the hospital is given to people with no training in taking care of patients. They want to take care of the business, and they are linked most of the time to the bottom line and not to patient care.

A competent physician or a good nurse enjoys his or her work; a bad one has no business taking care of patients. The top-performing physician is not invited to join the administration as CEO or CMO. Why?

A busy physician is a "cash cow," so why would a hospital move him or her into an administration role, thus losing their money machine? This is the reality of today's healthcare. Maybe a busy physician can be a good administrator, or maybe even better than the existing one!

Only at the end of his or her career can a busy physician transition to this role, but at that time, it may be too late. The implementation of oversight and good policies and metrics can make a lot of money for the hospital by saving on fees and penalties; we are talking about millions of dollars. But nobody counts that. Good throughput and no penalties for quality according to the value base purchasing rules can make a big dent in the hospitals' expenses and make then very financially successful.

Therefore, leading the hospital are businesspeople with little or no healthcare training who are making decisions for the physician. They buy instruments, medications, etc. without even talking to the physicians.

The physician, therefore, feels deprived of his or her autonomy and decision-making in healthcare, and most of the time needs to practice under a pretense and in a very unstable quality base facility.

Physician Leader

Unfortunately, physicians are highly individual persons who value their freedom and independence, but perhaps—paradoxically—embrace a highly structured and traditional learning process. They adopt this process because it is essential in providing them the tools for "success." Success is often defined in highly personal terms that involve the external recognition and validation of their achievements. The highest level of achievement is one that involves service to "others" rather than to oneself. But on the other side, physicians do not always like to work with other physicians unless they recognize the value of the collaboration.

Over the past century, medicine progressed successively from an art to a science. As scientific knowledge exploded in the 20th century, the "healing art" of medicine came to rely less on the relationship between physician and patient and more on the drugs and diagnostic tools the physician had at his or her command. Insights gained from careful physical examination and longitudinal observation of a patient decreased in importance as diagnostic tests became more accurate and less invasive. A prime example of this is the CT scan, which is ordered in many emergency rooms before the patient is even examined by a physician. Improvements in technology have also allowed physicians to successfully treat many patients who would have died in the past. Operations which were inconceivable a few decades ago are now commonplace, and new technologies are rapidly developing. Society and physicians individually now expect "medical success" as routine and are less understanding of "medical failures". This has paradoxically decreased satisfaction with medical care at a time when its potential to for good has never been higher. The second consequence of this technological revolution has been the demise of care that was centered on and controlled by the individual physician and, for the most part, occurred in the doctor's office, and the rise of "team-centered care," which is often located in the "medical center" with advanced diagnostic and therapeutic capabilities. The modern medical center, where annual mortality rates are routinely in the 1%–2% range, is a far cry from the hospital of the first part of the 20th century, which many patients viewed as a place to come to die. These contemporary organizations are highly complex, embracing inpatient and outpatient care, and generate both large amounts of revenue and expense. Such organizations cannot exist without a significant administrative infrastructure to support them. As healthcare became more complex and expensive, health insurance assumed greater importance. A discussion of factors contributing to the rise of the modern healthcare system is beyond the scope of this chapter. Suffice it to say that current healthcare insurance has effectively inserted itself between the doctor and his or her patient. Indeed, the terms "doctor" and "patient" are often replaced by "healthcare providers" and "healthcare consumers" in common parlance. Healthcare is often spoken of as "a right and not a privilege." It is worth noting that most "rights" are taken for granted, while most "privileges" are highly regarded and treasured. It is difficult to overemphasize the impact of this phenomenon, either economically or psychologically, on both patient and physician.

One of Us: A True Story

In this section, I would like to give an example of how administrators set up a physician practice, and how this represents an impossible victory for the hospital, healthcare system, physician, and patients. I will play a scenario, which happens every day, using Clark as the main character.

Clark is an experienced surgeon, just starting in a new hospital. After the first day, he comes home and is talking to his wife, a lawyer. "What do you call a practice that is hiring you for an excellent salary, doesn't provide any patients, doesn't do any marketing, doesn't set up any clinics, has very few ORs and a two-bed ICU, and whose staff have difficulties understanding how to treat patients? That is an impossible victory; that is a sign of disaster. What do you call this when you sit with a board member and the board member tells you 'you are supposed to sit in the office, you are never available.' And your answer is 'but I'm on call every day, and my name is in the emergency room as a surgeon; you call a surgeon when they are needed in the emergency room, on the floor, in the OR, in the office. They don't have to sit in the office. One sits in the office in a family practice, where patients sometimes walk in, but surgeons are different, they don't have walk-ins.' How can you explain this to a board member? I was sitting with three board members, two men and a woman, and we were discussing performance. The issue was that the surgeons didn't sit enough in their offices, and I said 'why do I want to sit in my office when I don't have an office.'"

Clark took a deep breath, and then he described his office: "I have a closet that was assigned as an office, no window, just room enough to walk in and out and not even a place to put another chair, and what I am going to do in the office, being a surgeon? People don't stop in front of a medical office and say 'Hey, by the way, I need my gallbladder out.' Their next comment is like, 'Oh but you are too focused on doing medical administration.' And I am looking at the board members like 'Do you know that your office manager doesn't even know the difference between a clinic run by a family physician, internal medicine specialist, gastroenterologist, or surgeon?' And I don't think that they understood what I was saying, and then on top of that, they told me that I was sitting in my office waiting for the patient to walk in. At that point, my answer was simply, 'Then, I think you need a medical officer to explain to your staff and the other people how to run a hospital.' What is the difference between surgery, medicine, and family practice? What do you call a practice where a physician is leading the group and is never present, and when he is present, he talks the talk, he promises and promises and never delivers? That is an impossible victory, and when you challenge this person a little bit more, showing that you can do everything, the next answer is, 'Oh, we can't work together.' This is an impossible victory. How can you explain that to a physician who is your peer and who is supposed to understand that you have time to do the surgery, time to see the patient, and also time to do the administration? It is not true that you are more valuable in the surgery, so you can make money for the hospital, of course, rather than writing policies and making sure that the quality is up to par, which nowadays is the most valuable thing in the hospital. It doesn't matter how much money you create in surgery, because the money that you make by ensuring the quality is given the opportunity to have a correct paperwork charge for Medicare or Medicaid; you don't have any withdrawal or any percentage that Medicare will remove from your numbers at the end of the year. What do you call it in a hospital when the CEO is a nurse, and all of a sudden she gets a promotion and she goes from the CEO to the COO job? That is not a promotion. The CMO was even more clueless, and instead of fixing the problems, he got rid of all the physicians by dismissing the physician's practice, which was composed of a specialist and one family physician … maybe he should have known that he should have more family physicians and one specialist!"

Impossible Victory

We have described an impossible victory. This situation could happen to one of us, in a common situation where a physician has to work every day. You can be accused of not having enough relative value units (RVU) when you don't have patients coming to the clinic; you don't have enough family physicians in town; you don't have enough nurse practitioners in town. How can it be possible that a specialty clinic can see more patients than a family practice clinic in a city that has a lack of family physicians? How is it possible that you can set up practice when nobody knows that you are in town? How is it possible that the marketing needs to be done in the name of the company and not with your name, so nobody knows who you are, and if they don't like the company, they indirectly don't want you. How is it possible that your first marketing was 3 months after you started? How is it possible that you don't even have a key to your office for 2 months to enter and do your charts? Unfortunately, there are no more question marks. Now those are clear points. When you have all this coming to your practice, it is an impossible victory. Run away before the corporation of the day decides that you are not a valuable physician because you don't make enough money for the hospital. The real question is who did the SWOT analysis before hiring you, who ensured the board—the corporation board, the hospital board—that hiring a physician would be a positive thing, a remunerative deal because you have enough patients to support the practice? Those people that did the SWOT analysis, those people that approved your position, those are the ones that need to be fired and not you for being accused that you don't see enough patients when there are no patients. If you have experienced any of these situations, please, run away.

Chapter 14

Healthcare Exclusivity Service, Charges, and Reimbursement Ratio

Exclusivity for Physicians

According to data from the Medical Group Management Association (MGMA), physician compensation accounts for 37% of total collections, or $186 billion (7.5% of total US healthcare spending).

We need to talk about the cost for a physician and the price of insurance. Reimbursement is secondary to a contract and the charge by the hospital.

Everything is inflated and then discounted, but patients see the gross charge, not the actual charge, and they think that the physician is making that much money.

That is why physicians have tried to open their own hospitals, since technical fees were much better than professional fees.

Money from the state and region etc. to pay on-call physicians has been used by the hospital, and not to sustain medical practice as happens for "border" funding in Texas.

Hospitals are skimping on paying on-call physicians while overcharging on the bill. In the same town, different hospitals have different charges. It is like running a restaurant that charges different prices for the same food, but the one that costs more had the better chef (physician). In some of these hospitals the chefs (physicians) are the same but the prices change. The chef is paying high dollars not the physician to work only in one hospital; the physician is not paying enough to have exclusivity—they need volume, which can go against quality.

You cannot hire just any physician and charge like a surgeon for open chole-cystectomy only, which is out of date, and for a standard that is the same as for a surgeon trained in laparoscopic surgery. Then, the hospital publicized they have a physician and they do not care if he or she has received the specific training. Physicians are expected to do magic just because are in town, but they do not provide support services or have magic wands to solve the problems.

Every hospital believes they have the best facilities, but I can do surgery in an underdeveloped country as well in their hospital; what makes the difference is the service available to the physician and not just to the patient. These services, combined for patients and physician, go hand in hand, and can strengthen themselves if used in combination.

Hospitals think that just having a surgeon in town will increase the number of surgical cases. Wrong—having the service first and the surgeon second will increase this; if there is no service, no surgeon will perform more complicated surgery or surgery in sicker patients.

Service Charges

The service charge, usually used in the hospital, is a charge that is determined by the different insurance providers. The cost, in fact, can change between Medicare and a private company, and very minimally. Lately, most insurance companies have been trying to standardize their payments to Medicare. In individual states, the amount of the charge is 110%–120% of Medicare. In particular areas, it seems like it is 80%–90% of Medicare, that is, below the Medicare cost. Unfortunately, in the medical profession nowadays, the charge does not represent the complete personnel cost, hardware cost, software cost, internal cost at the location, and so forth. These are allocated according to what the insurance will pay. As you can see in Table 14.1, this charge is based on specific numbers that represent a procedure (CPT code) or a specific type of diagnosis (ICDM code). These are set and are very well standardized. The charge is for the surgery itself or the surgical consult. The worst part of the business situation, at this point, is that the surgeon cannot charge anything for 90 days after the charge for surgery. Which business will see you for 90 days for free?

Table 14.1 UCR Charges by CPT Codes

CPT Code	Procedure	Medicare	Commercial Insurance
CPT 47562	Laparoscopic cholecystectomy	$601.88	$995
CPT 49505	Inguinal hernia, reducible	$429.19	$600
CPT 43846	Gastric bypass	$2,000	$4,500

There is no chance of getting any more payment for the service that you render. I wonder why physicians are upset and depressed?

Cost and Explanation of Benefits

One of the first things we learn is to start our business analysis from the Explanation of Benefits (EOB), and the EOBs received from managed care companies. An EOB is a document needed by the insurance company for the payment of the service delivered. Insurance companies commonly refer to this as the UCR fee profile. This profile has developed the use of Medicare resources based on a relative value scale (RBRVS) payment system, fees accompanied by the Health Insurance Association of American (HIAA) and, many times, with the internal methodology developed by the specific insurance company. The review of the EOB and managed care EOBs provide the practice with the comparison of what is being charged by the practice for a particular service or a CPT code and what is established to be the UCR by the third-party payer. Apparently, any situation where the practice is being reimbursed close to or at 100% of the charge indicates that the fee for the CPT price is too conservative. Managed care payers would pay the lesser discount rate or what they bill. Hopefully, this can make costs between 20% and 50% less of what indemnity payers will pay. If they charge a month, and it is less than the payer's discount fee rate, the EOB will show the entire billing as proof of payment. This is the significant indicator that these bills have problems since the practice's usual fees are less than the payer's discounted price. As a part of the fee schedule analysis, we should include and conduct studies utilizing a relative value scale. The relative value scale (RVS) is what was developed initially in California in the 1960s. The present Medicare fees are based on a relative value scale called a source based relative value scale (RBRVS), which was developed by Harvard University. Another value scale is the corresponding value for physician (RVP). The relative value is determined by factoring specific evaluation of the work including the time and skills required to perform the procedure, the risk of the process, and whether it is related directly to the procedure.

The Practice Chronic Problem

The first problem that the physician faces is that we have a very bad EOB that is not kept updated, and therefore our Accounts Receivable (AR) medium range is more than 100 days. We would like therefore to

1. Restructure our EOB
2. Look into our RVP for Medicare and Medicaid procedures, and contract with private insurance companies

3. Reconsider some of the CPT codes to increase the charge of 10%–15%, which will bring us closer to normality for the standard fee for a procedure

To achieve all of this, the manager or person in charge would have to be astonishing, and their objective will be that we keep the fee schedule continuously updated. The fee schedule analysis objectives are to make sure that the practice is not losing revenue as a result of low fee schedules and to ensure that the fee schedule is consistent and in line with the reasonable standard within the market area. Since the fee schedule is a significant part of the profitability of medical practice, it should be included in a practice assessment. It is imperative that we try to work toward accounts that have the potential for generating the most cash flow into our practice. It seems to me that, in a large organization, such as a state organization, most of the bills are paid according to what the highest bill is in AR (accounts receivable). This is based on the amount of AR. I think that doing it like this will lose a lot of money, as well as the possibility of collecting the small fees which have aging AR. The point of this is that if this number is aging for too long, we are missing the opportunity for collecting, particularly from state and federal organizations. Going after the significant accounts of AR is an excellent solution to get quick cash, but it is still not solving the problem. To be aggressive with AR is a good practice, but to lose on a small AR is also going to bring the practice into debt.

Cost and Multiplier

Being a specialist in this healthcare environment is not an advantage since the payment from the insurance company does not take into consideration your level of skill and ability. There is no adjustment for risk comorbidities, which are increasingly present in the patients we treat. A modifier of the code is in place, but give crumbs for much higher risk.

The system of relative values simplifies and ranks the procedure by comparing one CPT code to another. The higher the relative value, the higher the payment for the month of that procedure. For instance, a midlevel office visit (code: 99213) has a corresponding value unit of one, and an appendectomy (CPT code: 44950) has a corresponding value unit of 12. The more costly the procedure, the higher the relative value CPT code will be. Therefore, the CPT code 44950, which is supposed to pay $150.00, should be multiplied by 12 for a total of $1800, but unfortunately never happened. This number is supposed to be what the physician is reimbursed for the appendectomy. This will account for the technical skills, the complexity, and so forth. Another example is for the office outpatient visit. The highest office patient visit for us surgeons is CPT code 99205, which correspond to comprehensive/high complexity visit-evaluation. We usually charge $90.00, and the complexity RVP is 14. Therefore, the practice's commercial factor (CF) is about 6.43 (obtained by dividing the charge by the number 14 of the RVP).

An Example of Reimbursement in Surgical Practice

We know that, for a county hospital, there is a local geographic practice cost index (GPCI) component. The GPCI is Medicare's way to adjust the rate for the practical locality. The GPCI could be included or excluded from the IVU, but has usually been added to decrease the cost of Medicare in the area from which the hospital has to accept patients. What I would like to know is whether my surgical cases are reimbursed appropriately for the amount of work and training that I spend working on them.

I tried to locate our most common CPT codes and come up with our conversion rate. For example, I took a laparoscopic cholecystectomy (CPT code: 47562), inguinal hernia reducible (CPT code: 49505), and gastric bypass (CPT code: 43846), since it is one of the most common operations that I do.

The UCR charges for sample procedures are reported in Table 14.1.

According to MGM numbers, the conversion factor for surgical cases can vary between 120 and 260. Our conversion factor for this CPT code is supposed to be 124 for laparoscopic cholecystectomy, 124 for an inguinal hernia, and 164 for laparoscopic gastric bypass.

By dividing each CPT code by the dollar amount that we charge, we find our reimbursement ratios, as reported in Table 14.2.

Considerations

It appears that the RR rate is quite low in the practice. The RR for the cholecystectomy and the inguinal hernia is below 5 in three out of four calculations. For the CPT codes 47562 and 49505, this should be at least 10 or above. The RR for gastric bypass for Medicare is way too low. Without even knowing these data,

Table 14.2 Reimbursement Ratio: Conversion Rates to CPT Codes

CPT Code	Procedure	Medicare	Commercial Insurance
CPT 47562	Laparoscopic cholecystectomy	4.85	8
CPT 49505	Inguinal hernia, reducible	3.45	4.84
CPT 43846	Gastric bypass	12.2	27.4

most of the private practice bariatric surgeons have been declining operations on Medicare patients since they do not make enough money from them. As we show in our study, the reason is that the conversion factor is too low to approach such a challenging and high-skill-requiring surgery.

A good RR for bariatric surgery should be in the 30s. The CPT code for gastric bypass is specific to open surgery. To increase our charges, we should use the CPT code modifier for the laparoscopic gastric bypass, 43846. Doing this, the reimbursement goes up to 30%. The problem is that the laparoscopic procedure requires even more skill, and therefore the RR is higher: 258, since it is considered the most difficult laparoscopic surgical case. Consequently, the ratio between the reimbursement and the conversion rate is 23.25! This is even lower than the precedent ratio!

Therefore, there is a low reimbursement ratio according to our CPT codes. This is an unfortunate problem for any physician. Maybe the financial decision is to eliminate the procedure with the lowest RR. But who, then, is going to take care of the patients?

Where the Money Goes: True Stories

Although most of the population think that the money goes to the physician, unfortunately, as we have shown, healthcare is not in the hands of the physician. Let's take an example that everybody can understand, instead of speaking in political jargon. If you have gallbladder surgery, an elective gallbladder surgery, you come in the morning and you go home the same day for a cholecystectomy that is now done as a laparoscopy. You receive a bill of about $17,000–$20,000. How do you read this bill? It is challenging, because it is difficult to read, but the bottom line is, that out of this $20,000, only $350.00 or less goes to the surgeon and $300 goes on anesthesia. So, the question is, where is the big money going? And that is where the confusion starts, because people don't even read it. So the reality of the deal is that one bag of normal saline, which is salt water that is administered to the patient during surgery, can cost up to $500. Purchasing that same bag costs less than $5. If you take one pill of Tylenol for fever or pain, that one pill of Tylenol costs $7 or more, when with the same money you can buy 200 pills in the pharmacy. So is the system broken? Definitely! And nobody understands the real numbers. Similarly, if you have an appendectomy, this is a common procedure. The bill for an appendectomy? About $10,000–$11,000. How much do the people that do the work make? The physician, $150 dollars, and the anesthetist, $300. What is the difference here? The patient most probably came to the emergency room, so you have this exorbitant charge from the emergency room.

Some of this is direct experience from my wife's gallbladder surgery, where a Tylenol tablet cost $7, a bag of saline $150 dollars, and the same-day surgery

$17,000, while neither the surgeon nor the anesthetist charged anything. The funny part is that I was working at that hospital! Talk about preferred treatment!

Suggested Reading

1. Wikipedia. Explanation of Benefits. Available at: https://en.wikipedia.org/wiki/Explanation_of_benefits.
2. Vineet Arora, Christopher Moriates and Neel Shah. The challenge of understanding health care costs and charges. *AMA Journal of Ethics* 17: 1046–1052, 2015. doi:10.1001/journalofethics.2015.17.11.stas1-1511.
3. Faith Asper. Calculating "Cost": Cost-to-Charge Ratios. *ResDAC*. Available at: http://resdac.umn.edu/sites/resdac.umn.edu/files/Calculating%20Cost%20-%20Cost-to-Charge%20Ratios%20(Slides).pdf.
4. David Muhlestein. 2013, July 15. What Types Of Hospitals Have High Charge-To-Reimbursement Ratios? *Health Affairs Blog*. Available at: https://www.healthaffairs.org/do/10.1377/hblog20130715.033072/full/.
5. Robert Smoldt, Denis Cortese, Natlaie Landman, and David Gans. 2017, January 21. Medicare Physician Payment: Why It's Still A Problem, And What To Do Now. *Health Affairs Blog*. Available at: https://www.healthaffairs.org/do/10.1377/hblog20170127.058490/full/.
6. Jeff Bendiz, Rose Schneider Krivich, Keith L. Martin, Chris Mazzolini, and Todd Shryock. 2017, December 25. Top 10 Challenges Facing Physicians in 2018. *Medical Economics*. Available at: http://medicaleconomics.modernmedicine.com/medical-economics/news/top-10-challenges-facing-physicians-2018.
7. Beth Jones Sanborn. 2016, December 16. Cash Flow, Reimbursement are Biggest Challenges Facing Physicians in 2017, Survey Shows. *Healthcare Finance*. Available at: http://www.healthcarefinancenews.com/news/cash-flow-reimbursement-are-biggest-challenges-facing-physicians-2017-survey-shows.

Chapter 15

Who is Controlling Healthcare?

The Doctor is Out: Insurers Controlling Healthcare

To introduce this subject, I will use the experience of Edward Volpintesta,[1] as published in February 2015:

> I was not on the UnitedHealthcare Medicare Advantage plan, and he had to choose a different doctor. This was just the latest blow from modern medicine as it creates distance between patients and doctors. The human element in medicine is being lost. I think we've lost it already. A little over a year ago, UnitedHealthcare summarily dismissed me along with more than 2,000 other Connecticut physicians from its Medicare Advantage Plan. This was done presumably to protect its profits by eliminating those doctors who did not follow their rules, which are supposed to protect their profits.

As a result, thousands of patients had to find new doctors. Some of them had long-standing relationships with their doctors who they trusted.

There were a few more among our other patients who said they were being forced to find a new doctor. Others may have left but felt embarrassed about having to go elsewhere and just quietly stopped coming.

Volpintesta then concluded:

> UnitedHealthcare's concerns about protecting its profits are much more significant than its concerns about how much patients rely on

their regular doctors. It takes years to build trust and confidence; and finding a new doctor to replace the one with whom they had a long, comfortable relationship is a worrisome and challenging task for many of them. This is only one example of what can happen when insurance companies amass too much power and dominate the health system, controlling physicians and patients. The president of the Connecticut State Medical Society in the January issue of the state medical journal pointed out that doctors, more than anyone else, have a better understanding of what their local communities need and that their voices must always be heard in shaping health care policy. The time has come for our lawmakers to tell insurance companies to back off. They must not be allowed to burden doctors with needless paperwork or interfere with their abilities to act in the best interests of their patients.

Medicare Administered by Private Insurance

People aged 65 and over are eligible for Medicare. Once, Medicare was administrated by the federal government only. However, there was too much work and too much fraud, so the health insurance companies convinced the federal government that they could help them.

Therefore, what happened is that Medicare is not administered by the federal government alone anymore but by the federal government through the insurance companies. A lot of insurers, both private practice and private insurers and for-profit insurers, now have Medicare plans. This has been a disaster because the private health insurance Medicare plan is not a real Medicare plan because the cost has been increasing, so by health insurance companies helping the federal government to administer Medicare, those companies are making even more money from the federal government.

The premiums are going up, and they are making Medicare part A, part B, part C, and part D: they are splitting this Medicare into many parts. Medicare, since it is one single payer, is supposed to have one plan where you get paid for your hospital treatment, you get your medication, you get the rehab, you get everything. It shouldn't be divided into three million levels in such a way that, for each level that you want, you have to pay extra. This is not Medicare anymore. This is private insurance administered by Medicare. If you notice, Medicare is not regulated by the federal government, but if you see, your Medicare is managed by the different private health insurance companies that administer the same health insurance before you are 65 and then they take over Medicare after you are 65. Therefore, there you are back with the same health insurance company.

Insurance companies help the federal government to govern Medicare but not the people!

Obamacare

How did the insurance get paid after Obamacare? Obamacare was a disaster for the health insurance companies for their bottom line. So, what did they come up with? They increased the premium of the people that could pay. That is why the bonus for the middle class has been going up. The incentives for people who get health insurance from their jobs is going up. There is more money to be paid as the deductible every year, and this increases the copayment. Why do the copayments go up? So health insurance companies don't lose the money administering Obamacare to the people who need Obamacare. The health insurance company looks at their bottom line. To make a profit, a profit they increase the premium of the other people because it is impossible that the cost went up rapidly as soon as Obamacare was in place. It is impossible that the United States (US) spends three times more in healthcare than everybody else, and it is impossible that in the US we have sick patients because they don't take care of themselves and they wait for health insurance. There is no plan for preventative medicine; there is no plan to decrease medication, there is no plan for anything. I present an example here to make this even more evident.

Why do we pay $7 or $10 for Tylenol pills when we go to the hospital? Because your $10 dollars doesn't pay for your pills but pays for the other 200 tablets that are administered to people with Medicare or to people that don't have insurance. Therefore, hospitals and health insurance companies don't lose money—they get the money from the people who don't have any choice but to pay.

Since they have insurance, they pay the expenses of the other people who use Tylenol. So, your one pill of Tylenol buys Tylenol for 100 people, and the game that the hospital plays is the same game that the insurance company plays. If you go to the hospital, you have insurance; you pay a high premium because your premium is going to cover the other three or four people that have Obamacare.

They can go to the hospital and get their care, of course at a lower rate, which is not similar to your rate, but you are the person with the insurance, you are middle class, you are blue-collar class, you pay for everybody else. This is not because of Obamacare. Therefore, there needs to be a better distribution of the general wealth, and the price of healthcare needs to be decreased for all.

Social System

I grew up in a place with a social healthcare system, as does everyone outside the US, so I am very familiar with this type of system; it has always been taken into poor consideration. First of all, in a social system, there is the real freedom of choosing a doctor which we don't have in the US unless you have money, as we have discussed previously. Second, you don't have to worry if you don't have money, as you will still be taken care of.

Is the care under the social system the best? No, because of course, having one payer, the federal government, means that the system is not great. Look at the VA. The VA provides care for everybody, but it sometimes takes 2 or 3 weeks to see a doctor at the VA. But you know what? The people get seen, the people get the job done, the people get the support that they need. The federal government pays, of course, and there is one payment. But you can have private insurance at the top, as in the US. So, you have a basic service for all, and an extra service, with a cost, for those who can afford it.

How does it work? You can buy extra, private coverage in Europe or South America or Asia, so if you are sick you can go to the same hospital, but the same hospital also provides a semi-private or private service where you pay extra to the doctor. It is, in reality, a mixed system. The wealthy still can choose their hospital and doctor, but the needy can have a basic service without fees. The middle class can have medical care without selling their homes. The level of care in a university hospital is as good as you can have it, performed by the same physician who also works half of the time in the private arena.

That is the same thing that happened here, without paying insurance every month if you do not want to. So, if you are sick and you go to the hospital, you can get treatment for free. If you want better service or you want a private clinic and so forth, you might spend, let's say, $8,000 or $9,000 to get your surgery done.

The physician is happy because of instead of getting 50 or 100 bucks, he gets maybe $1,000 or $2,000, and the patient is satisfied because he or she has received excellent service. Everybody is happy, and everybody makes money appropriately and accordingly to the job that they are doing.

The same thing has happened in Mexico and in every other social system so, if you have money as in the US system, you can have other healthcare on top of your social network in a single payment. If you don't have money, you still have the individual pay that protects you, and I think this was missed by Bernie Sanders' concept of one single payer. He does not understand—he did not explain the extra care that you can get by building a private system on top of a single-payer system. In Mexico, the patient pays the physician and the physician contracts the hospital, so the hospital is much nicer to the physician because physicians have become their payers. Here, the physician is considered a secretary.

Real Finance Evaluation of Yearly Healthcare Cost

Let's do some financial evaluation. If you pay $1,000 a month in insurance, you pay $12,000 a year. Plus you have to add your copayment and the initial payment you have with your insurance policy, which varies from $3,000–$5,000. Taken together, this will cost you almost $20,000 a year. Well, if you pay 28% in taxes, this means that you make $150,000 a year or more. $20,000 is one-seventh of your salary. If you add those costs and translate the cost of taxes to expenses, this means you pay 35% or more in taxes! In a social system, you pay close to 40% in taxes, and you do not have to worry! Is not better? It is like going on vacation and instead of buying your meal you have an all-inclusive deal. You pay more, but no worries! Healthcare should be an all-inclusive situation like the vacation resort!

Why does the US not see the simple economics instead of protecting its territory? There was a time that Americans wanted to migrate to Canada for medical service. Why? To get worse service? No, in Canada, Europe, and Asia there are top doctors and hospitals, even in Mexico if you know what you are choosing. People come to the US because its healthcare is well organized, it has money for research, and new machinery. In the US, if you are wealthy, you can get any treatment, even if you are not a US citizen.

Lifetime Expenditures Math without Political Influences

This is a report of the real situation, without political and corporate influence. Most people, when bombarded by different data, try to protect their health insurance because a lot of money goes to their campaign and therefore they don't want to talk about the potential of having a private system on top of a single-payer system. But let's go a little bit further. If you look at the money that you spend on insurance, let's say $500 a month, it means $6,000 a year. If you are an average person that started paying for health insurance, let's say at 20, by the age of 40, so 20 years later, you have spent $120,000. By the age of 50, you have spent $180,000. By the age of 60, you have spent $240,000. By the age of 70, you have spent $300,000. So an average American, who starts getting insurance at 20, spends an average of $300,000 in health insurance, if not more, in a lifetime, depending on the plan they have, how many babies, etc. So, isn't it better to have a system that keeps the $300,000 in your pocket, and where those that have the $300,000 can either buy private insurance independently or, if they need $10,000 to have surgery because they don't have insurance, they can pay the extra $10,000 and they have better care in a private clinic with a doctor that smiles every time. In the end, not everybody spends $300,000 on healthcare but the insurance company takes this $300,000 in your lifetime and makes a million out of it, which is not fair, so the money that you invest in healthcare, not reinvest in healthcare, they disperse in health insurance. One more. If you spend $6,000 a year or more, which is $500 a month, it means that you have to add that $6,000 to the money that you spend in taxes. Let's say that you make $100,000 a year and you pay average taxes of 25% or 26%, so basically, to make it easy, let's say 25%, so you are paying taxes of $25,000 plus every month. You pay for your Medicare, your Medicaid. If you look at your check, every month a Medicare and Medicaid plan is listed. Therefore, you pay for your single payer, you pay for other people off insurance, not for your insurance. On top of that, you pay $25,000 in taxes so, at the end of the day, you pay $25,000 in taxes, and you pay Medicare and Medicaid, so you have another 2% or 3% of your taxes. You pay $6,000 for health insurance, which out of $100,000 is another 6%, so if you consider this all as taxes, your total tax is 33% or 34%. For people that make $200,000 or more, if you do the same calculation, it comes to 40%–41%. Now, my dad in Italy was spending 41% in taxes every year, but when he got sick with Alzheimer's disease and needed a PEG, he got to the hospital, he got to rehab, he got to everything, and we didn't have to pay exorbitant costs, just 30 euro ($40) a day. It is nothing, because in the US if you go to rehab, sometimes out of pocket, it can be $5,000 a month versus what we spent—800 euros, which is $1,000 a month. It is impossible to live in a system that charges six times more for the same service because sooner or later the system is going to crash, and I agree with Senator Graham that Medicare and Medicaid are going to crash and this is reported in another chapter.

Medication Costs

For medication, in a social system, you pay about 10–15 euros for most medicine. Here, if you don't have insurance, God help you if you can't afford the medication. Now, if you can't afford the medicine and we are in a free country, why can't you buy the medication in Canada or Mexico? Because if you do that, or a physician does that, it is going to be reported and he or she is going to lose his or her license for trying to help a patient to get the medication, and those medications are not second-class medications—this is what the public doesn't understand.

These are medications produced by the same company, which sells the same medicine at a different price in different countries. I can go to Canada and Mexico and buy the same medication for one-tenth of what I pay here in the US, but people don't see it. Why do people in the US go to Mexico or Costa Rica to do their dental work? Because with $400 or $500, which here is only your total copayment, you can get the full job done. Why is it better to go to Mexico to get your appendix done?

Because in the end, it costs you the same as here with insurance, so not only do you pay the insurance, but you pay the same price that in Canada and Mexico they pay for the whole thing without insurance. As an example, some people that I know in Mexico make $1,000 out of gallbladder surgery, while we make $350 for a gallbladder in the US. Is that fair? How do they do that? Because in Mexico, for instance, the system is different. The patient pays the physician, the physician then pays the hospital; that is why the physician can make a little bit of extra money, but he or she is in the concept of healthcare to pay the physician, they do the job on you. Why do we have an intermediary that gets the money and who decides how much to spend on the physician, and then complains that the physician is not as good, the physician doesn't want to work, why is the physician burned out? Because they have no control of the system, so maybe in Mexico they are smarter than in the US because, actually, who gets the money? It's the physician, not anybody else. The patient trusts the physician; the patient pays the physician; the physician takes care of the patient. Isn't that what healthcare is supposed to be?

I know a doctor who orders chemotherapy medication from Canada to help his patients who cannot afford the high costs in the US. The companies reported him because he was using non-FDA-approved medication (same meds from Canada, just with a different brand name, sometimes even from the same company). He lost his license, and some patients may have died for lack of treatment! Good job society! Protect your margin at the cost of human life. That is why healthcare needs to be in the hands of the physicians, as they are the only ones who provide care, and they do care.

Note

1. Edward Volpintesta. 2015, February 6. Insurers Coming Between Doctors and Patients. *Hartford Courant.* Available at: http://www.courant.com/opinion/op-ed/hc-op-volpintesta-doctor-patient-insurance-0208-20150206-story.html.

Suggested Reading

1. Sudip Bose. 2017, August, 29. The High Cost of Prescription Drugs in the United States. *Huffington Post.* Available at: https://www.huffingtonpost.com/entry/the-high-cost-of-prescription-drugs-in-the-united-states_us_59a606aae4b0d81379a81c1f.
2. Aaron S. Kesselheim, Jerry Avorn and Ameet Sarpatwari. The High Cost of Prescription Drugs in the United States. *Journal of the American Medical Association* 316(8): 858–871, 2016. Available at: https://jamanetwork.com/journals/jama/article-abstract/2545691?redirect=true.

Chapter 16

Healthcare Reform: The Never-Ending Story

Debate

I was watching the Cassidy–Graham debate on reforming, repealing, and changing Obamacare. As is usual after such a conversation and after the discussion hosted by CNN, people were more confused than clear. It is complicated to understand healthcare by understanding the political jargon, how much money is used for this, how much money is used for that. It is interesting that the two Republicans that proposed this new law are both doctors yet it seems by the way that they talk that they are not doctors but are politicians, because neither of them pointed out what the real problem is and where the real money is going. It is interesting also that during this debate, the most precise person was Bernie Sanders. His plan will not work because it is too extreme for the United States, but maybe there are some points that he doesn't see, and he does not understand how extraordinarily well the social system works in other countries. Instead of always saying how the reform is going to work, why don't we understand what is happening at the basic working level and not in Washington.

CBO: Graham–Cassidy Would Increase Uninsured 'By Millions'

The latest Senate Republican bill to replace the Affordable Care Act (ACA) would reduce the deficit by at least $133 billion over 10 years, but at the cost of increasing the number of uninsured Americans "by millions," the Congressional Budget Office (CBO) said on September 24, 2017.

The CBO said that it would need several more weeks to provide more specific estimates on how the bill would affect the federal budget, health insurance coverage, and premiums for plans sold in the marketplace, or exchanges created by the ACA. It issued the preliminary study at the request of the bill's chief sponsors, Senators Lindsey Graham (R-SC) and Bill Cassidy, MD (R-LA), who were aiming to change everything. Under a budget resolution enacted by the Republican-controlled Congress, their ACA repeal-and-replace legislation can't be filibustered and needs only a simple majority for passage. But there was the risk of not having enough votes to overcome a filibuster by their unified Democratic colleagues.

The CBO based its analysis on the first version of the Graham–Cassidy bill, which had been amended since then to make it more fiscally generous for states represented by reluctant Republican Senators. However, the report was enough to swing Sen. Susan Collins (R-ME) over to the "no" column, where she joined the late Sen. John McCain (R-AZ) and Sen. Rand Paul (R-KY). As it stood, bill sponsors didn't have the minimum 50 votes needed for passage (Vice President Mike Pence would supply the tie-breaking 51st vote).

The Graham–Cassidy bill takes money earmarked by the ACA for Medicaid expansion, premium and cost-sharing subsidies for exchange plans, and the Basic Health Plan that states can implement under the law and will distribute it to states in the form of block grants between 2020 and 2026. The CBO said that the bill reduces the deficit mainly because the new block grants would be smaller than the various ACA subsidies for healthcare. The difference is partly offset by the repeal of the penalty for the individual and employer mandates, which would yield about $200 billion in revenue between 2020 and 2026.

The threshold of $133 billion cited by the CBO represents the savings achieved by the ACA repeal-and-replace bill passed by the House earlier this year.

The projected increase in the ranks of the uninsured could vary widely, the CBO[1] said, "depending on how states implemented the legislation, although the direction of the effect is clear." The agency ticked off three main reasons why the bill would leave more people uninsured:

- Enrollment in Medicaid would decrease because of "large reductions in federal funding" for the program
- Lower subsidies under the bill would depress enrollment in individual health plans in the exchanges
- Repeal of the penalties for the individual and employer mandates would erode enrollment in all types of health insurance

These enrollment dips would be partially offset by people signing up for new insurance programs created by states with block grant money and "somewhat higher enrollment in employment-based insurance," the CBO said.

Is the System Broken, and Where?

Is the system broken? Why don't we fix the system and understand where the money is going, instead of trying to fix healthcare reform? There are too many stakeholders with interests other than patient care. Pharmaceutical companies, and now healthcare corporations, are in business for the margins. So what is happening to the most critical stockholder, the one who provides healthcare: the physician?

How Physicians Are Paid by the Insurance Plan

Let's understand how the physician gets paid. If you are a physician in the US, you can of course charge whatever is reasonable. Sometimes it can cost $100 for a visit, but the physician gets the discounted fee of less than 50%. So, if you are a physician out of the plan, you can charge, let's say, $100, and then you submit the bill to the patient or the insurance company. You send the statement to the insurance company, who will deny it because you are not part of their plan, and then they submit it to the patient. So the patient gets stuck with $100 bill, and of course, it is hard to pay. Therefore, the patient will be very careful next time they go to the hospital to be seen by a doctor that is in their insurance plan. But what does it mean to be in the insurance plan? They need to accept the rules of the insurer. Either you agree with those plans, or you are out. The patient, therefore, is going to look into the physicians that are under the insurance plan and only use those physicians. Therefore, at some point, the physician, if he or she wants to survive, has to get into the program and accept this low and sometimes ridiculous reimbursement for his or her job. Why absurd? Because, for instance in primary care, the physician is paid for the time spent with the patient—let's say 20 minutes, but after this time spent with the patient, the physician has to arrange for laboratory tests, for a CT scan, for an ultrasound, maybe for a referral to another physician. Therefore, the 20 minutes is not 20 minutes, but instead it is 40 minutes that the physician spends working on a patient. Those extra minutes are not paid; the insurer refuses to reimburse the actual time and reimburses only the face-to-face time, stating that the nurse could do some of the other jobs. True. But who is paying the nurse in your office? You! So, if you don't get paid for non-face-to-face time and she does not get paid for her job, you, not the insurer, pay the nurse. It means that the physician is not getting paid for the time he or she spent taking care of the patient, but only for the discussion with the patient. Now, consider this at the lawyer level. If you talk to a lawyer, if you send an email to a lawyer, if you have a question for the lawyer, if you send a memo to the lawyer, he or she charges by time, not by face time but by real time. So, why can a lawyer charge by real time but not a physician? Because the lawyer has a direct connection with the client. The client pays the lawyer directly, unlike the physician who gets paid by the insurer. The insurer acts like an intermediary and takes a cut of everything that happens and tries, of course, to maximize its margin.

Insurance Plans

If a physician is in an insurance plan, this means that he or she accepts that plan and agrees with the reimbursement of the insurance, even if the amounts are ridiculous, as stated previously. Therefore, the Republican side in particular has stated that the US has the best healthcare plan because individuals are free to choose any physician they want. This is not entirely true. Yes, they can choose any physician they want in the US if they have the money to pay the out-of-state, out-of-town, out-of-network fee, and a large copayment of up to $10,000 a year. That is not freedom, because if I don't choose the physicians that are on my plan, it means that I pay extra money. It is free for people who are wealthy and have money, but it is not free for everybody. Therefore, the freedom in the US is on a different level. We still think that we have democracy in healthcare. Of course, those making the laws don't care because they have federal coverage, which is very different. So, this freedom is not freedom. No, it is a dictatorship. You can choose every physician in a booklet of physicians that the insurance company sends to you as a patient. If you select any physician outside of the pamphlet, you start paying. Of course, you can choose any physician. This does not happen in a social system, I repeat, does not occur in a social network. In fact, if you are in Canada, you can choose any physician in Vancouver, in Toronto, in Montreal, and it's the same plan, it is a national federal plan. If you are in Italy, you can go to Milan, or you can go to Sicily, it is the same plan. That is freedom of choice, which is not what is present in the US where the insurance company controls which physician you have to choose. Otherwise, you can see any physician, but you pay extra. Is this what they mean by freedom of choice? There is freedom of choice only for the wealthy, not for everybody.

Impossible to Collect the Fees

There is another point that the general population does not understand. When we have a patient that comes for treatment, and we want to charge his or her insurance, the insurance company puts up a lot of barriers to payment. For instance, they start delaying the payment, 30 days, 60 days, 90 days, 180 days. And if you don't have somebody in your office that continuously calls the insurance company to try to get paid, you probably don't get paid because after 6 months, the bill goes into oblivion. So not only do you have to track the bills, but you also have to hire somebody in your office to monitor the statements, meaning a new person, new insurance, and a new salary, which accounts for more than $60,000 at the end of the year. Then, if you give your bills to a collection company, it makes between 7% and 10% of your collection, as those people are going only after the big bills. They don't go after the 20-, 30-, 50-, 100- dollar bills, which at the end of the day, adds up to more than one bill of $1,000. Therefore, you lose money on that too. The system is not strong enough to protect the physician. The insurance company now has a rule of requesting a call for a pre-certificate. The physician needs to have a pre-approval of coverage if specific labs or an x-ray or a particular procedure are needed, and that takes forever. Sometimes, not only do you have to hire somebody to do all the pre-approvals, so another extra person, another $50,000, but now you are also paying $200,000 for an assistant's salary, but he or she is not helping enough. The physician needs to talk directly to the insurance representative physician about the insurance. What that means is a lot of wasted time for the physician, who needs to make phone calls while he or she is busy seeing patients, busy doing his or her job, and working to take care of the patient. Not only is this a broken system, but it becomes almost impossible to get in touch with this special insurance physician in charge of approving specific procedures.

It is one of the worst experiences the physician can have. Because if the surgeon calls for approval of the surgery, the physician on the insurance side is a pediatrician or is in family practice, and is never a surgeon. Sometimes a cardiologist calls, and it is still a pediatrician; sometimes a neurosurgeon calls, and it is still a pediatrician or a family practice physician. Now, I don't want to offend the pediatrician or the family practice physician who works for the insurance company, but he or she doesn't understand what the procedures are and what the needs are, because he or she is not in the same specialty. So not only do you have to make extra phone calls, you have to hire additional people, but the person that the physician has to talk to get a pre-approval is not in the same specialty, and therefore it is quite impossible sometimes to have a discussion at the same level, so then what happens? It is not approved, because the physician on the insurance side is not in the same specialty and his or her job is to pass as few as procedures as possible.

Skimping the Dollars

It seems like I am talking about things that are from another world, but these are typical things that physicians face every day. Does it look like we are incorrect about insurance companies? No, it's not true. I have friends who work for insurance companies; they were surgeons, they were in internal medicine, and they told me that their bonus is based on how much money they save the insurance company, which translates into how many approvals they deny to physicians and hospitals. That is what they do. They refuse as much as possible, they close as many loops as possible, to leave the physician without the appropriate charge or the hospital without their application fee. That is their job. Therefore, they work for the insurance company, they work for getting the bonus, and they don't care about their fellow physicians, and I think the same thing happens when they go into politics—they forget that they were physicians at one point. Just between you and me, look at the health insurance CEO, he or she makes 2, 3, 4 million dollars a year, and who pays for that salary? The people that pay the insurance; your premium is not going to pay the doctor, your premium is going to pay all these administrators that work for the health insurance and the 3 million dollars of the salary of the CEO. That means that the insurance company cannot pay all the claims. What that means is that to get the 2 or 3 million dollars, they should save as much money by not actually paying the provider that takes care of the patients who trusts the insurance company to take care of them. The money that the insurance pays is not going to the doctor, it is not going to the hospital, it is going into the pocket of the insurance company, who gets more and more prosperous because most insurance is for profit. I remember when I was in one of the towns on the east coast, going to one of the primary insurers in this country, and at the office of this insurance company, there were three fountains. I mean three fountains are quite impressive, it seems as though you are in Hollywood, but if I tell you that the fountains had a plate of gold on the bottom, that is bad. Not even in Saudi Arabia can you get three gold fountains in your office, so how were those fountains paid for? Think about it!

Decreased Physician Salary

Then the question should be, "OK, so how much does the doctor make?" A surgeon's salary has gone down 50% or more. Now, on the east coast, there are states that pay less than $200,000 for a surgeon. But they pay $180,000 for a nurse practitioner or $220,000 for a CRNA, who still works shifts and passes the complicated issues to the physician. In the West and Middle East, they pay $300,000 and less now. According to data from the American College of Surgeons, the surgeon produces about $2.2 million for the hospital, with a mere 300 cases a year or fewer. Therefore, they earn only 10% of what they generate for the hospital. Is that ridiculous? Absolutely! And the salaries are getting lower and lower. Not only are there lower and lower wages, but there is an increased cost for running the practice, and the electronic medical records system costs a lot of money and needs to be changed or updated every 2 or 3 years because, in the US, we have a million medical records. Medical records companies speak different languages, and they do not talk to each other. The medication, the prescription, everything now costs. Who is paying the price for this healthcare? The cost of this healthcare is funded by the provider that sees their money cut every day, despite the increased cost of insurance. So the problem is not to stop the price of insurance from increasing, the problem is to talk to the insurance company who has created a system where the only one that makes money is that health insurance company!

We need to create a system that works, eliminating the bureaucracy. Healthcare insurers have excellent control over the network. Hospitals have become incorporated to defend themselves from this system of insurance.[2] The physician is not allowed to do the same, since bylaws are in place to prevent this.

Unfortunately, to create fewer expenditures, the hospitals are spending less money on supplies, and paying less money to the doctors and nurses at the end of the day. This fight between the health insurance companies and the hospitals is killing the country's healthcare, as they are destroying our ability to provide healthcare to the patient.

Notes

1. Avik Roy. 2017, June 27. CBO Predictions About The Senate Health Care Bill Are Deeply Flawed. *Forbes*. Available at: https://www.forbes.com/sites/theapothecary/2017/06/27/cbo-predictions-about-the-senate-health-care-bill-are-deeply-flawed/#2f8c62eb79d4.
2. Healing Health Care Requires Bold Action. *Winnipeg Free Press*, 2017, June 14, p. A9.

Suggested Reading

1. Jessica Banthin. Health Care Spending Today and in the Future: Impacts on Federal Deficits and Debt. *Congressional Budget Office*. Available at: https://www.cbo.gov/system/files/115th-congress-2017-2018/presentation/52913-presentation.pdf.

CORPORATE HEALTHCARE

Chapter 17

Corporation Interferences and Compliance

The Chronic Crisis of US Healthcare

Rebecca Jasso-Aguillar[1] and her coauthors have found that crucial decisions about privatization and the entry of multinational corporations into the public sector occur at the executive branch of government level, including the Office of the US Trade Representatives and the Department of Health and Human Services. For instance, in late 2001, US Congress approved "fast-track" authority for the executive branch to enact international agreements in trade for healthcare and other services. In other countries, the Ministry of Health and the Ministry of the Economy are connected.

Navarro[2] pointed out that the US healthcare industry and health reforms enacted between 1980 and 1994 opened the door to for-profit hospital chains in the delivery of health services since the 1980s, shifting healthcare to the for-profit sector and their benefit. This approach is decreasing or eliminating nonprofit insurance companies.[3] This involvement was facilitated by federal policies and programs such as Medicare, which provided about one-third of the revenue for the nonprofit organizations. The government paid for but did not control the delivery of health services and provided subsidies representing a significant proportion of overall health expenditures. Therefore, the government lost control a long time ago! The only justification was the crisis in health services in the 1980s. The medical-industrial complex acquired influence by financing members of Congress sitting in powerful committees that drafted health legislation. From 1981 to the first half of 1991, insurance political action committees (PACs) contributed about $60 million to congressional campaigns. At the same time, the medical professional, pharmaceutical, and hospital PACs contributed, respectively, $6 million, $28 million, and $9 million.

The number of uninsured has increased to over 44 million people. As Adiga puts it, America's privately managed healthcare system has created a substantial financial burden for millions of seriously ill patients and middle-and lower-income families.

Despite the penetration of managed care in the US, HMOs have tackled a declining rate of profit and have reaped significant earnings by initially paying hospitals a fixed capitation for each patient at a low negotiated rate.[4] The profits went down as the market became saturated by HMOs.[5] By 1996, private health insurance premiums were rising at a much lower rate than MCO costs. Reasons for higher costs included rapidly increasing prices of medications; greater bargaining power for doctors and hospitals, as they have consolidated; and a sicker population.[6]

In 1997, the managed care industry was struggling with higher medical costs, insufficient premiums, Medicare costs that were more substantial than expected, and an increasingly competitive market.[7–10]

Therefore, HMOs decided to merge to get a better bargaining position. The incorporation of Wellpoint Health Networks and Health Systems International, for example, led to the control of about one-sixth of California's 12 million HMO enrollees, "a size that could drive hard bargains with doctors and hospitals in the competitive California market."[4] When Prudential HealthCare put its health unit up for sale, its 4.7 million members made it "an attractive acquisition candidate if anything to keep it out of the hands of someone else."[9] Aetna's 1998 acquisition of Prudential made Aetna, according to its press release, the country's largest provider in health benefits, with approximately 22.4 million members overall and 18.4 million members in managed care.[11] This type of story appeared all over the US, creating a strong insurance hold and weak healthcare.

Examples of Physician Conflict with the Healthcare System

The medical literature abounds with a variety of controversial issues linking physicians and the healthcare system, too many to address in a single chapter. Here, we have listed some of the more current and controversial issues that challenge physicians in their relationship with the ever-changing healthcare system.

Cost of Obtaining Adequate Care for Patients

As the health insurance industry has increased in size and power, it has been able to impact on medical care by the ability to pay for or deny benefits for specific procedures and conditions. Inherent in the creation of some healthcare products, such as

HMOs or PPOs, is the need for cost containment and efficiency. In applying this to the sheltered lives which they insure, healthcare insurers have not paid for some services and procedures that the physician may deem necessary for the treatment or prevention of a medical condition.

Therefore, there has been a persistent denial of preventive medicine and screening tests by some insurers, which ultimately may be more cost-effective but does not bring any short-term reductions in expenses. *Healthcare should start as prevention, not as an intervention.*

Many healthcare insurers have the same constraints of profitability and growth that other private industries do. This sometimes forces the healthcare insurance industry to choose between what expenses they can cover, which in the case of preventive medicine often is removed from the budget. In some cases, it has required legislation to force the health insurance industry to provide necessary screening and prevention procedures such as a colonoscopy.

Physicians can be put in an awkward position if recommending a particular procedure or treatment, which they feel is essential for the appropriate care of the patient, when the patient's insurer will not cover that expense. Also, physicians who work for organizations that provide health insurance products are constantly informed of the need for cost containment and the payment of therapy. They can be discouraged from making appropriate out-of-network referrals or from prescribing necessary treatments due to the lack of cost containment. In some cases, physicians derive direct personal benefits (i.e., salary bonuses), which are based on the profitability of the providing organization. The inherent conflicts in this situation are apparent. Issues regarding the coverage of benefits have required litigation to achieve resolution.

Corporation Compliance

Corporate compliance is a difficult concept. The reason it is difficult is that the idea bases its status on multiple regulations and various laws. It is not easy to comply with all of the legal and governmental requirements in the current practice of medicine. For instance, the reimbursement of Medicare service is regulated by 1,756 pages of federal law, 1,257 pages of interpretative regulation, and 14,277 pages of manual instructions to interpret those regulations. I do not know if anybody will read these lengthy regulations to understand how to practice. I am sure that most of the physicians get these regulations through either their manager or the business office to make sure that they comply with all of the rules. Unfortunately, there are a few things that are important and need to be clear.

1. The office of the Inspector General, which is part of the Department of Health and Human Services, issues all of the regulations and then checks on those rules.

2. The False Claims Act is very important because it also involves the false claims.
3. In 1996, the Health Insurance Portability and Accountability Act (HIPAA) was developed into the Medicare integrity program.

Other agencies have been created—in 1992, with healthcare reform, Congress approved the HIPAA, and from this, all of the rules and regulations of medicine were applied. This is very important to know because non-complaint individuals have received fines of between $5,500 and $11,000 per incident for false claims filed. Also, there privacy rules that are regulated by the HIPAA, and people can be sued civilly when non-compliant with these rules. There are many government agencies combating fraud including the Department of Treasury, the Department of Labor, the Department of Justice, and the attorney general. One of the most critical areas of compliance for medical malpractice is to code and bill correctly. If you do not know how to do this, it is probably better not to code at all; otherwise, you could violate the Medicare fraud law, and after a few episodes, you could lose your license. Physicians might choose not to participate in a federal program such as Medicaid and Medicare because they are not allowed to bill this agency for services rendered to the patient, which is very important. Also, physicians that "dump" patients inappropriately, for instance in the emergency room, can be reviewed and adequately punished. Because of this, rules and compliance are needed. Therefore, the US Federal sentencing guidelines have put in place several important directions, including written policy and procedures covering

1. Compliance
2. Compliance monitoring
3. Comprehensive training education for staff members
4. Internal control and auditing
5. Establishment of open lines of communication to identify potentially fraudulent activities
6. Protection against improper actions
7. Investigating and disclosing of violation

Compliance for Physicians

These seven points are now part of implementing a program of compliance. All physician offices have to have these points in place. The hospital office has to continuously check that these rules are followed. Compliance is an inter-disciplinary effort that crosses all of the boundaries inside a practice or hospital. To establish compliance, you need an officer, a checklist, and somebody in the office itself to follow up and make sure these points are continuously updated and observed. A compliance policy manual is usually best developed internally by the compliance officer by working with other members of the practice or the hospital who might possess knowledge of a specific area, such as coding and billing. A training session needs to be put in place because education is one of the things that the federal government requires.

The topic of the training session is usually a consequence of noncompliance, a brief review of fraud and abuse, and an analysis of the elements of compliance, particularly in the place of work. It is most important to have an open discussion about problems or concerns and a feedback policy so that the compliance officer will know of any issues. The best indicators to monitor are usually the long-term number of claims denied, the comments in the medical records, and the CPT full code usage by code and physician. These are probably the most important. For clinical success, the complaint process will demonstrate that your practice is dedicated to compliance. Comprehensive review systems should be maintained, and documentation should be retained of the education material, receipt of a compliance manual, correction given, resolution by the physician over the governing body regarding compliance, and goals and minutes of staff meetings. All of this comes under the policies and procedures of a physician practice compliance program. The most important of these are compliance and performance improvement, compliance communication, compliance guidelines, legal responsibility of staff, and conflict of interest. There are probably 20 that need to be followed. The bottom line is that we, as physicians, need to establish a compliance risk assessment mechanism and a compliance performance improvement process. We need to be careful not to have a problem with fraud regarding billing, such as quoting a particular code showing that the physician was present for the whole procedure instead of the resident. Medicare can call this fraud because a procedure done by the resident is much slower, and therefore, according to Medicare, the academic institution needs to implement and police the policy. We need to be careful to bill correctly and to be present during the procedure to comply with the Medicare rules.

Notes

1. Rebeca Jasso-Aguilar, Howard Waitzkin and Angela Landwehr. Multinational corporations and health care in the United States and Latin America: Strategies, actions, and effects. *Journal of Health and Social Behavior* 45: 136–157, 2004.
2. Vicente Navarro. The Politics of Health Policy: The U.S. Reforms, 1980–1994. Oxford, UK: Blackwell Publishers, 1994.
3. Carol A. Caronna. Filling the Gaps in the Managed Care Story: The Organizational Field Approach. *Journal of Health and Social Behavior*. 45: 26–58, 2004.
4. Milt Freudenheim and Clifford Krauss. 1999, June 16. Dancing to a New Health Care Beat; Latin America becomes ripe for U.S. Companies' Picking. The New York Times. Available at: https://www.nytimes.com/1999/06/16/business/dancing-new-health-care-beat-latin-america-becomes-ripe-for-us-companies-picking.html.

5. Karen Stocker, Howard Waitzkin, Celia Iriart. The Exportation of Managed Care to Latin America. New England Journal of Medicine. 340: 1131–36, 1999.
6. Ron Winslow. 1997, October 28. Oxford to Post First Quarterly Loss Ever—MCO's Stock Plunges 62 Percent; Forecasts for 4th Period, Year Also to be Missed. The Wall Street Journal.
7. Johanna Bennett. 2001, January 15. Managed-Care Firms Taking Pulse: Few Surprises are Expected in the 4th Period Earning Reports. The Wall Street Journal. B.11C.
8. Susan Pulliam and Ron Winslow. 1997, October 9. MCOs Costs Woes Unsettle Wall Street. The Wall Street Journal. C1.
9. Leslie Scism. 1997, October 2. Prudential May Sell Off Health Unit. The Wall Street Journal. B11.
10. George Anders and Ron Winslow. 1997, December 22. Turn for the Worse: HMOs' Woes Reflect Conflicting Demands of American Public—Many Expect Lower Costs But Special Treatment; The Street Turns Sour—Lack of Realism all Around. The Wall Street Journal. A1.
11. Aetna Inc. Business: SEC Filings and Reports. Lexis-Nexis Academic Universe; 2001. Form 10-K, for the Fiscal Year Ended December 31, 2001. Available at: http://www.aetna.com/investors-aetna/assets/documents/2017/4q17-form-10k.pdf.

Suggested Reading

1. Aetna Inc. Aetna International, Inc. Signs Letter of Intent with Servicios Financieros, C.A., S.A.C.A. 1998a. Retrieved 20 December 2002. http://www.aetna.com/news/1998/pr_19980115.htm
2. Aetna Inc. Aetna Sees Rise in Commercial HMO Medical Costs—Trend To Negatively Impact 2Q Earnings. 2000a. Retrieved 20 December 2002. http://www.aetna.com/news/2000/pr_20000718.htm
3. Pierre Bourdieu. *Acts of Resistance: Against the Tyranny of the Market*. New York, NY: New Press, 1998.
4. Holly S. Buchanan, Howard Waitzkin, Jonathan Eldredge, Russ Davidson and Celia Iriart. Increasing Access to Latin American Social Medicine Resources: A Preliminary Report. *Journal of the Medical Library Association* 91: 418–25, 2003.
5. Lawrence P. Casalino Unfamiliar Tasks, Unsettled Jurisdictions: Describing the U.S. Health Care Market. *Journal of Health and Social Behavior* 45(Extra Issue): 59–75, 2004.
6. CIGNA Corp. Business: SEC Filings and Reports. Lexis-Nexis Academic Universe, 2002. Form 10-K, for the Fiscal Year, Ended 31 December 2002. Retrieved 20 May 2003.
7. Healthcare Dream for Insurers: Will Social Security Changes Lead to Major Surgery on the Medical System? *Financial Times*. 23 October 1997, p. 6.
8. Mary Jane Fisher. Managed Care Plans Exit Medicare. [Electronic version] *National Underwriter* 104(28): 1–2, 2000.
9. Bruce M. Fried and J. Ziegler. The Medicare + Choice Program: Is it Code Blue? 2000. Retrieved 12 July 2002. http://membership.hiaa.org/pdfs/000608codeblue.pdf

10. Louise Kertesz. The New World of Managed Care. [Electronic version] *Modern Healthcare*. 3 November 1997, 115.
11. Allyson M. Pollock and David Price. Rewriting the Regulations: How the World Trade Organization Could Accelerate Privatization in Health Care Systems. [Electronic version] *Lancet* 356: 1995–2000, 2000.
12. Howard Waitzkin. *At the Front Lines of Medicine: How the Health Care System Alienates Doctors and Mistreats Patients ... And What We Can Do About It*. Lanham, MD: Rowman and Littlefield, 2001.

Chapter 18

Corporation and Physician Dissociation

The Texas Medical Association (TMA) handed out a questionnaire in Texas about corporation-physician dissociation. The following data were taken from the TMA webpage and the presentation was given during the annual meetings.

The questionnaire contained multiple items, but we will focus on the one related to physician practice, quality, and employment.

Poor Care Quality Due to Hospital or Facility Practices

Thirty-six percent of physicians have witnessed specific cases in their practices in which the quality of patient care was adversely affected by the policies or operations of a hospital or surgical facility. Physicians who saw damage to care quality were most likely to report inadequate and inconsistent facility staffing (64% and 54%, respectively).

Adverse Quality of Care and Physician Employment

The question was: Have you seen cases where physicians lost employment, contracts, or hospital privileges because of corporation interference?

Twenty-three percent of respondents saw cases where physicians lost employment, contracts, or hospital privileges after raising issues about hospital regulatory compliance or patient care quality, and 35% of physicians were concerned it could happen to them.

In the past, there have been some differences in age in respondents who have seen these cases:

Thirty-two percent of physicians in the middle of their career (between 40 and 60) as 22% of older and 14% of younger age physicians gave this answer.

For the question on whether they were concerned that that would happen to them directly, the most relevant physician respondents were surgeons (47%) and indirect specialties (53%), while pediatricians were 31%, primary care 27%, and nonsurgical specialties 33%.

That was it. There were no statistically significant differences by county or practice type.

Poor Care Quality Due to Third-Party Payer Practices

Respondents were asked to report whether they saw specific cases in which the quality of patient care was adversely affected by the policies of a managed care plan or government program. A majority indicated that, in the past year, there was at least one instance in their practice in which patient care quality was adversely impacted by a health plan (73%) or Medicare (52%). As noted, the impact was greater in the private sector.

Cause of Adverse Impact by Third-Party Payers: Physicians who saw care quality problems were asked to report the reason or reasons for the adverse impact. The most frequently identified cause varied by the payer.

- Managed care: Respondents who witnessed quality problems in health plans reported that issues were caused by formulary limitations and treatment denials (55%).
- Medicare: Medicare quality problems were most frequently attributed to limited or tiered formularies (40%) and treatment denials (34%).
- Medicaid: Quality problems in Medicaid were most frequently attributed to formulary limitations and inadequate access to specialists (38%).
- Workers' compensation: Among physicians who saw specific cases of care quality problems in workers' compensation, treatment delays were the most frequently listed reason (16%).

Issues between the Hospital and the Physicians

For the question regarding whether poor care quality was due to hospital or facility practices, 36% of physicians witnessed specific cases in their practice in which the quality of patient care was adversely affected by the policies or operations of a hospital or surgical facility. Physicians who saw damage to care quality were most likely to report inadequate and inconsistent facility staffing (64% and 54%, respectively).

Adverse Quality of Care and Physician Employment

Twenty-three percent of respondents saw cases where physicians lost employment, contracts, or hospital privileges after raising issues about hospital regulatory compliance or patient care quality, and 35% of physicians were concerned it could happen to them.

How Much Is Controlled by the Corporation?

I asked an old physician friend of mine, who practices during the year in the US and has seen the different stages of healthcare, about the question of how much control the healthcare system has. He answered, "Total and absolute control. It is like a dictatorship with repercussions. It is like Russia with the KGB, always ready to investigate and punish". That was shocking and revealing at the same time. I asked other physicians the same question in private conversation, and they all—in similar words and form—described the corporation expansion in healthcare as a regimental system, where the Generals (the bosses) were people having less background training than them and a cultural background that had minimal understanding of clinical medicine and its problems.

For fun, for a while, I asked all the CEOs, COOs, and CFOs what background they had. Manufacturing was number one, followed by psychology, laboratory and hospital techs, and pharmaceutical representatives. Now, how can these people understand the clinical scenario? Manufacturing does not produce a human being, and the patient-physician relationship cannot be classified as a bunch of rules and punishments. Hospitals and laboratory techs working in healthcare will continue to have two types of contact with physicians: (1) Fear. The physicians do not talk to them well or (2) Revenge. They try as much as possible to keep them under their toes to satisfy their revenge when they were techs. This way, the hospital will never grow. There are nurses in administration, which will create an environment favorable to nurses, of course. But where are the physicians and their representatives? Changing the CEO will not change the problems, while changing the culture to bring people together will!

The Physician Is Lost

The physician now is lost and ready to get out of practice, looking for different jobs in various fields. Some join the administration field, but they have multiple layers of non-clinicians in front of them and to get high in the pyramid they have to conform and lose their physician's touch.

Most important perhaps, is that the business model imposes its hierarchy, which is neither physician- nor patient-centered. While it may seem that CEOs of many corporations are imperial or even despotic, their underlying obligation is to better the organization. Failure to do so is virtually the only grounds for their dismissal. They have a commitment to the organization, not to the patients. The tension between physicians and healthcare organizations is further increased by the fact that physicians are not highly valued (at least in their role as physicians) in many of these organizations.

What Physicians Think about Corporations and Corporations about Physicians

Since the reader may think that this book contains only the author's perspective, I would like to report another physician's side. In this case, I was interested in the tweet by John Mandrola MD,[1] on October 2017. He said:

> The monthly productivity report based on relative value units (RVUs), include your productivity also comparing to doctors across the country. Clinical works get you a bunch of RVUs. Listening to patients, examining patients, counseling patients, or hugging patients earns very few RVUs. Doing the important research, teaching colleagues, and reading the medical evidence deserves zero RVUs.
>
> Too often, in too many medical systems, RVUs have become the primary unit of success. If you have good electronic health records and good and always completed documentation and you see a lot of patients, you are valuable. If you like to spend more time with your patient and be more conservative than you cannot be valuable. God save you if then you are thoughtful and frank about silly policies, you become an outlier. If you do these things, and the RVU does not reach the 75% of the standard bar, then you are out. Imagine educators whose paychecks are determined by the number of RVUs they generate rather than the bedside skills they impart to learners. Productivity and RVU have no place in medical care. There needs to be a different system of valuing the care of people with the disease."

Doctors Hired by Companies

> Hoping to curb rising health-care costs, some companies have long wished they could choose their workers' doctors, with an eye toward cost-effectiveness without sacrificing quality. Why not, then, hire physicians for the company and encourage employees to use them?

A few large employers—Gillette, Southern California Edison, and Goodyear among them—are doing just that, with some success. And given the widespread frustration over the cost of medical care, many others should also be interested according to Thomas R. Burke, a principal at A. Foster Higgins & Company, a benefits consulting firm in Washington. Mr. Burke, who was chief of staff at the Department of Health and Human Services in the Reagan Administration, argues that the concept would mainly help employers with many workers in a community that lacks a desirable health maintenance organization. But bringing about such a program can be challenging.[2]

The concept is best suited to companies with many employees in an area, as they can be challenging to organize. Winning employees' confidence can be fierce because of skepticism that the employer might have a conflict of interest in that it wants to hold costs down. A senior official of the American Medical Association, Dr. James S. Todd, said: "The arrangements are reasonable as long as doctors are not forced to cut costs at the expense of appropriate care." Isn't this what is happening every day in hospitals?

Healthcare Industries Push Doctors to Do More

Physicians Are Getting Tired

Megan O'Rourke[3] said:

> Why has it become so difficult for so many doctors and patients to communicate with each other? A physician's job is technologically proficient but emotionally draining. The medical system is inconsistent, that is best for treating acute, not chronic, problems. For instance, there are countless cases of substandard care, overlooked diagnoses, bureaucratic bungling, and even outright antagonism between doctor and patient. For a system that invokes "patient-centered care" as a mantra, modern medicine is startlingly inattentive—at times actively indifferent—to patients' needs.

The pressure of increasing and achieving quality care, dealing with autocracy, and the time spent on cumbersome electronic medical systems really place doctors in a stressful situation. The responsibilities are there, but the recognition is gone. The loss of control of healthcare, which is now with the nonmedically trained staff, makes physicians frustrated and in need of finding alternative hospitals or alternative jobs.

Notes

1. John Mandrola. 2017, October 17. A Corrosive Force in Medical Care. Available at: http://www.drjohnm.org/2017/10/a-corrosive-force-in-medical-care/.

2. Glenn Kramon. 1989, July 11. Business and Health; When Companies Hire Own Doctors. *The New York Times*. Available at: https://www.nytimes.com/1989/07/11/business/business-and-health-when-companies-hire-own-doctors.html.
3. Meghan O'Rourke. Doctors Tell All – and It's Bad. *The Atlantic*. 2014. Available at: https://www.theatlantic.com/magazine/archive/2014/11/doctors-tell-all-and-its-bad/380785/.

Suggested Reading

1. Updated TMA White Paper Delves into Corporate Practice of Medicine Doctrine. TMA. 2016. Available at: https://www.texmed.org/Template.aspx?id=43708.
2. Corporate Practice of Medicine. AMA. 2013. Available at: https://www.ama-assn.org/sites/default/files/media-browser/public/about-ama/councils/Council%20Reports/council-on-medical-service/i13-cms-report6.pdf.
3. Ken Ortolon. The Corporate Practice of Medicine. *TMA*, 108(4): 49–52, 2012. Available at: https://www.texmed.org/CPMwhitepaper.

Chapter 19

Moving Out of Healthcare

Getting Entrepreneurial

Christina Farr[1] made a nice point on physicians changing jobs: "It's a challenge to quantify the exact number of doctors moving out of the health care into the tech world. Even if a large physicians' group like the American Medical Association (AMA) tried to keep track, it would need to determine whether to include doctors that advise startups but still practice one or two days a week or just those who have left medicine altogether. I suspect that the former category is much more extensive. ... the migration of doctors into the health tech space is noticeable."

It is now fairly common for well-funded health-tech startups to have medical directors, physician founders, or chief medical/health officers on their team. Some high-profile examples include Collective Health, Sherpaa, Startup Health, Doximity, Aledade, and AthenaHealth. And the AMA tells me it is proactively forging partnerships in Silicon Valley and beyond to help doctors "work in tandem on the innovative tech solutions that promise to change health care."[1]

Web-based companies, manufacturers, pharmaceutical companies, and other organizations have catered to doctors with experience in high-tech and brought the problems to the surface.

Some California-based doctors started a private Facebook group called "dropout docs". The group included Rebecca Coelius, a UCSF medical school graduate who worked as a health director at Code for America.

Other members included Amanda Angelotti, a fellow UCSF graduate who works in clinical systems design at One Medical; Sean Duffy, a Harvard Medical

School dropout who co-founded Omada Health; and Connie Chen, a practicing doctor who co-founded a chronic disease management app called Vida. This highlights the problem that doctors have today: To be or not to be a doctor? This is the question many have asked after years of training and extensive payments for college loans.

Present society has been increasing the push for leaving healthcare. Some of the problems doctors face are

1. Depression
2. Loss of a goal
3. Loss of control in healthcare
4. Loss of recognition from healthcare administration
5. Loss of patient recognition, since doctors feel that taking care of patients is a "must" that they need to do, with or without being paid for it
6. Practicing medicine as a secretary, and the loss of the art of the medical profession

All of these issues and more have caused burnout and suicide to reach the highest rate ever, and doctors are getting tired and want to do something else.

Doctors Are Tired of Insurance Companies

Doctors hate insurance companies because they feel that they are often powerless when it comes to dealing with them.

The average physician insurance contract is written entirely in favor of the insurance company. The insurance company gets to decide what is medically necessary, how disputes are resolved, and how much the physician is to be paid. When it comes to payment, the physician, unless he or she is with a vast group, usually has very little negotiating power. Often the insurance company unilaterally changes significant contract terms with a single written notice to the physician that requires no independent physician agreement.

Insurance companies also affiliate or purchase other contracts. When this happens, a physician will suddenly be subject to a reduction in rates with a company he or she previously had no agreement with because he or she has a deal with another company. There is nothing that the physician can do in response to this except to seek to terminate the deal, which is extremely difficult to do.

Unionized to Be Protected: Nurse Example

It is getting closer and closer to the time when corporations will completely take over healthcare, and hospital nurses and, shortly, physicians will form a union as they have in other countries to protect themselves from the overwhelming influence of private companies and government and a lack of job protection.

In January 2016, nurses at Hahnemann Hospital, part of the for-profit hospital chain Tenet, voted to unionize with the Pennsylvania Association of Staff Nurses & Allied Professionals (PASNAP) by an 82% majority in a National Labor Relations Board election, winning representation for roughly 850 nurses.

The example was followed by hundreds more nurses at another Tenet facility, St. Christopher's Hospital for Children. Closing chronic staffing gaps keep workplaces and patients healthier.

California and New York States were the first to limit the number of patients a nurse has to care for during his or her shift to between four and six. This has been an achievement since, before the limit was introduced, in the same states, they were in charge of eight or more patients, which really cannot ensure a good quality of care. A similar situation has arisen in the ICU, where a nurse is required to take care of one or two patients, but in the same state in the US they care for four. This goes against the principles of the American Nurses Association (ANA). It is interesting that, when this limitation was applied to New Jersey and Pennsylvania, matching the nurse-to-patient ratio, "nurses' burnout and job dissatisfaction were lower, and nurses reported consistently better quality of care."[2]

Nurses aren't the only ones stretched to the breaking point in hospitals and clinics. Doctors are also pushed and reminded every day that they are workers like everyone else, and that it seems like everyone can practice medicine. We always forget that the only two professions having a license to practice in healthcare are doctors and nurses (nurses need to understand this too, and their importance in this battle).

A national study on doctors' work experiences has revealed massive work-related stress, with 46% reporting severe stress, up from 38% in 2011. One major factor cited was new regulatory pressures under the Affordable Care Act.[2]

A few overworked doctors have recently established a union of their own in Minnesota. An 11-member medical professionals unit of Steelworkers Local 9460, which includes three doctors along with nurses and other staff, recently finalized its first contract at Lake Superior Community Health Center, a facility serving low-income communities in Duluth, Minnesota. The hard-fought deal came after years of internal struggle. Staff complained of a climate of anti-union hostility and intimidation – tensions that culminated in a contentious organizing drive and 42 unfair labor practice charges.

Some changes made were removed several months later without any explanation. Unionized nurses are being fired for dubious reasons that are potentially fabricated. The same thing will happen to physicians if they demand better work conditions or even better equipment in the hospital. They automatically become a non-team member and therefore a "persona non grata."

For all medical workers, the term *overworked*, once a proud hallmark of the profession, is now rotten.

Michelle Chen reported:[2]

> To tackle the cause, nurses unions have become a leading voice in the movement for single-payer health care. Eakin argues that breaking the dominance of the medical insurance industry is critical for overhauling the social-service infrastructure as a whole.
>
> ... "We're in a strong position to advocate for all patients. But I think a lot of employers are trying to undermine that because they don't want nurses to be speaking out about inequality and about improving access for everybody."

Addressing inequality in all levels of the healthcare structure, as a workforce and public trust, means that patients aren't safe unless their rights at work are secured.

Eakin[2] said: "One of the biggest things we're going to get out of [a union] is a legal voice, and a way to raise our voices up together."

With the corporation breathing more and more on the necks of physician and nurses by requesting more hours, the same quality, and reduced payment, the idea of a union is no longer a mirage.

Notes

1. Christina Farr. 2016, April 24. Why So Many Doctors Are Advising Startups. *FastCompany*. Available at: https://www.fastcompany.com/3059231/why-so-many-doctors-are-advising-startups/.
2. Michelle Chen. 2016, August, 3. Nurses and Doctors Are Fighting Back Against Corporate Healthcare by Unionizing. *The Nation*. Available at: https://www.the-nation.com/article/nurses-and-doctors-are-fighting-back-against-corporate-health-care-by-unionizing/.

Suggested Reading

1. Meghan O'Rourke. Doctors Tell All – and it's Bad. *The Atlantic*. 2014. Available at: https://www.theatlantic.com/magazine/archive/2014/11/doctors-tell-all-and-its-bad/380785/.

Chapter 20

Peer Review for Physicians: What about the Administrator?

Professional Practice Evaluation

Each hospital has multiple policies in place to check on physician practices such as the Focused Professional Practice Evaluation (FPPE) and the Ongoing Professional Practice Evaluation (OPPE). The goal of these policies should be to establish a systematic process to evaluate and confirm the current level of professional competence. This evaluation process is known as "proctoring." Implementation of the proctoring method does not directly affect opportunities.

It is good to have physician practices monitored, but no local monitoring of administrative practices is in place. This leaves the CEO as the absolute captain of the ship, going to the COO and CFO if mistakes or wrong investment, etc. are made, without any supervision, since most of the time they act in agreement with the regional CEO, etc. Local people and physicians are unable to comment or have a say without being in danger of losing their jobs.

The problem is that this is creating a dictatorial system, and if you try to say anything, you will be persecuted through loss of privileges and block time, and a sham peer review, just to create a file, and finally, your contact may not be renewed.

This creates hatred among physicians and a system that will never work. Has any dictatorship ever worked in history?

Losing Physician Independence

In this new authoritarian system, the Medical Executive Committee (MEC) is at the mercy of the administration; fine politics are usually adopted to make sure that the chiefs of different specialties are supporters, and any that are vocal tend to be eliminated. Therefore, an MEC of "friends" is built and it can be manipulated by the CEO or others that may be present during those meeting. Their work usually is done before the meeting. Now, I know a depict a situation that many people and the hospital will reject as inaccurate, but is it not true?

Sham Peer Review

We have been witnessing an increase in sham peer reviews purposely done to punish the physician who is not pro hospital and pro administration. I have witnessed many in my tenure on the Texas Medical Association Physician Advocacy Committee. Despite trying to be as balanced and objective as possible, some of the hospitals' accusations were so ridiculous that, at the time, they seemed to be at the opera and not in a meeting. Passion, tragedy, and death look like the correct mix for an opera; unfortunately, in real life, we call that misery.

As Dr. Verner Waite[1] summarized:

> Professional peer review is intended to protect the public from incompetent or unethical practitioners. However, it could and often does remove the most honest, ethical, and competent physicians, to the advantage of unscrupulous competitors. The Health Care Quality Improvement Act (HCQIA), which was enacted with the support of the American Medical Association, immunizes false testimony, thus allowing gossip to be converted into testimony and depriving physicians of independent judicial review. The accused physician is often ruined financially. The victim must pay his legal fees, whereas his accusers are not responsible for any legal fees, which are paid by the hospital. The National Practitioner Databank (NPDB) transforms "disciplinary" actions into a professional death sentence. The abuse of the process, unfortunately, widespread.

One of the most challenging obstacles to overcome, other than physician apathy, is the reluctance of physicians to fight for one of their colleagues who is under attack. Again from Dr. Waite's article:

> It has been said that the hunted physician will find that the sham peer review process is a lot like hunting gazelles in Africa. Thousands of gazelles will be grazing peacefully on the plain. When a lion decides

to attack a chosen victim, most of the herd will continue grazing placidly as the surprised victim attempts to run for its life. Physicians of the pack just believe that bad peer review isn't their problem and will never happen to them. Most importantly, HCQIA and state laws that permit complete immunity for malicious and false testimony by sham peer reviewers must be overturned. Absolute freedom, like absolute power, corrupts absolutely. The peer review process needs to be fair and unbiased, and peer reviewers must be held accountable for their actions to ensure the integrity of the process. Finally, sham peer review needs to be labeled as such and exposed wherever and whenever it occurs."

Sham peer reviews are not a new problem. The *Pittsburgh Post-Gazette*[2] published a series of articles in 2003 on physicians facing retaliation after standing up for patient care. Many of the stories are related to sham peer review.

Most of the time, there is a chief medical officer (CMO) involved, but let's try to understand his or her position if the CMO is not aligned with the administration who decided that he or she is out, so the CMO needed to defend and protect his or her job.

How This Is Possible

How is this possible? Let's look at the director of the risk management department. In a small hospital, most of the time is not even one healthcare provider with a medical degree. Initially, directors were nurses and were thus in the "intelligent system," and were helped by physician supervision and/or a consultant to review the case before bringing it to the surface. I have been working with a lab tech that all of a sudden became the director of risk management. I have been working with nurses who worked all their lives in a hospice and then had to evaluate acute care issues. These people do not know about the pathophysiology of the disease, and therefore report everything that might be a sentinel event, even if it is not a sentinel event. It is all about disruption. The next time your case goes for review, of course, it is found to be nothing. So, the regular physician thinks that that was it. Wrong! That case stays in your file, even if it should not be there. During a stressful time, "the time of cholera" to paraphrase Gabriel Garcia Marquez, when there is a case that went wrong, all your old "files" are pulled out but not read; they are instead simply counted. Therefore, at that point, you have, all of a sudden, a number of files that might place you in trouble. With the excuse of peer review, this record is kept away from you so that you cannot even rebut or reply. Another case is where you do not go along with risk management; they will keep a file on you, knowing that sooner or later the numerosity will count, even though all your cases were in the perfect alignment with standard of care.

Administrators Need a Deeper Medical Background

Do you think the CEO will ever check? First, most of them do not know much about the clinic, and second, they prize the risk management people, as they like to have ammunition.

On the CEO side, it is incredible that most of them are entirely "ignorant," meaning that they ignore the clinical basis of healthcare, and the clinical team. They see numbers and hospital flow, but that is it.

I remember being accused by a CEO of not sitting in my office for 8 hours a day when he was paying me for 40 hours a week. Therefore, I was not available. Now, that was the month that I was on call in the emergency room for 29 days. What is wrong with this picture? First, he does not understand surgical practice. The surgeon does not sit in the office waiting for customers; that is what medical and primary care physicians do. The surgeon is on call. When you are on request, then you are available 24 hours to the emergency room, hospitals, and your clinic. People do not come to the office to ask to have their gallbladder removed. People need a referral. So you think that the CEO understands medicine and specialties? No, right? If he does not know this, how can you expect to build an excellent primary care base to feed the specialty doctors, including surgeons? Then you wonder why his hospital is doing poorly. Where is the control on him, where is the feedback he can hear? Maybe we should collect file on CEOs too, and when too many accumulate, we can fire them as they do to us. He was a lab tech that went to earn an MBA and got to be CEO. But in his mind and actions, he was and still is a lab tech.

Another example is along the same lines. I was talking to a board member, and she said the same thing to me about the 8 hours, justifying herself by saying that that was what the administration told her. She was and is a lawyer. I was trying to explain the situation to her, but you know, if the government told her then it must be true. So I concluded my meeting with her underlining that they need a CMO, at least he could explain to the state and her. She had too big a head to understand. Where was the problem? The CEO in the hospital changed; the one that hired me was gone, and the new one wanted different people and not me, and therefore she started a campaign to get me out, and she was successful. This CEO came with abysmal training in psychology from a small school and an MBA from an unknown college. My training and my understanding, both of healthcare and of finance, were way superior, but, well, she was the CEO, and I was just a simple surgeon.

Do CEOs Obey the Same Rules as Physicians?

I was working in the hospital, and the CEO was trying to do what he could. The issue did not reside in the CEO, but in the way the hospital was organized. The regional CEO did not want to change it—he set it up that way, and to change it would be to admit his failure. So, the CEO left, and a new one came along. The latter of these was let go from his old hospital, and we found out that he had had two DWIs; yes, he had a problem with alcohol and went to detoxification. This was not reported to the MEC when he interviewed. He got the job. Think about it—if he were a physician, he would have had his license suspended. Big difference. So where is the control over administrative hiring? After a short honeymoon period, he showed his character—he was smelling of alcohol in the morning, but nobody could report anything since they were afraid of the regional CEO. His personality, of course, was one of "You are hospital employees." Therefore, you are his secretary. Many physicians left, including me. He was able to destroy the little good in the hospital and drove everybody out, as he did in the hospital he was in previously. If a physician had that history, he or she would never be hired. He was right and all the others wrong. Even a surgeon nowadays cannot afford to have that attitude.

The bottom line is that the regional CEO was conveniently "moved" to another job, where he stayed until the new local CEO realized how bad he was and got him out. During that period, the only thing the organization was interested in was the financial profile. Nobody cared about the welfare of the nurses and physicians, which then affected the patient care; nobody was wondering why many people were leaving.

I do not know if you have noticed, but when a physician leaves the hospital, all of a sudden he becomes a lousy physician; when an administrator moves, he does so for a better job. They will never admit the problem with the hospital, and the cycle will repeat over and over.

Lifespan of a CEO

By published data, the lifespan of a CEO is 2.2 years. This is normal and accepted. If the physician moves every 2 years, everybody thinks that there is a problem with the physician. Why? We are both professionals! Why do CEOs leave? Some of them have no clue—they come and make a modification, and they lose money; some of them try to be the dictator, and neither the physician nor the firm can get him out; some of them cannot make financial plans, and they get replaced. I have seen a CEO, who was making good money for the hospital, decide to invest in buying property and land without anybody stopping him. He was in the patient care business, not in the realtor business. Lo and behold, the hospital went bankrupt and the board relieved him. People were not getting paid, and the hospital almost closed. But, as you know, hospitals cannot close because they take care of people, so the board was able to save it. If it was any other business, it would have been closed. The more tragic story is that that CEO found another job quite quickly and went on to ruin another hospital. If it were a physician having problems, he would never find another job, and he would undergo scrutiny from the hospital, boards, etc.

If we want to fix healthcare, we need to improve the level of our CEOs, who focus on healthcare even though they are not doctors!

How Many Points of Scrutiny Are There?

The point I want to make is that a physician has many levels of scrutiny and performance evaluation. However, the people that run the hospital, those that are the "boss" of the hospital employees and physicians, have no scrutiny of their knowledge, plans, goals, etc., as long as the financial sheet is in order and they make money for the organization. They do report to the board, which is usually formed by local people who do not know much about healthcare, and they are easily convinced by the CEO.

This is true also for the physician. I remember a surgeon who operated on everybody and experienced a lot of complications. The hospital knows, but they decide to ignore it because they were making money. But as soon as the surgeon is no longer "their friend," they call for a peer review.

I saw an oncologist give chemotherapy to a patient ready to die who did not need chemo at all. The hospital knew it but did not pass any comment since he was using the cancer center in the hospital and therefore he was generating lots of money.

I saw an ICU doctor keeping patients intubated for a week in ICU, thus increasing the patients' rates of pneumonia, tracheostomy, and UTI central line infection. The hospital knew, but nothing was done. Even after Medicare fined him $4 million, the hospital closed their eyes, and he continues to charge for a 40-minute ICU visit without seeing or visiting the patient. In reality, how can you see the patient for 40 minutes and run an ICU of 20 beds, an average hospital census of 30 patients, and a clinic of 40 patients a day?

Do Nurses Need Peer Review from Physicians?

The physician has to compete for patients, which is fine. Then they have the patient in the hospital, and those get whatever nurse is available. Whether the nurses perform well or badly, the physician can do nothing. Physicians tend to have their favorite nurses and favorite floor. Sometimes, if we cannot get a specific nurse, we will choose a floor where the manager is attempting to address our request and educate the staff.

Would it be better if a physician could choose a nurse? If that is the case, many nurses will be without patients. I know it sounds outrageous, but we as physicians must improve more than others, and we do not see the same in the nursing world. Some nurses do not want to develop—if they work on a medical floor, they do not want to take care of a surgical patient. If they are surgical nurses, they do not wish to care for a cardiac patient. But we can define the types of nurses. There are some that strive for excellence, while some are just there for their shift and do not care to learn or to observe, but instead only worry about the paperwork.

A nurse who is kind, available, and hardworking at one point will get tired because he or she is paid the same, and to be good they need to be "anal" and be strict. So he or she becomes less nice, while the nurse that does the minimal work and plays on her phone is "nice." There is no bonus or recognition for taking good care of the patient.

Why can physicians not evaluate nurses, and extend an opinion on their knowledge? Maybe that would help to identify those nurses who work better in one specialty than another. Perhaps a nurse does not get cardiology, but will make a tremendous surgical nurse, etc. If this process is not in place, the excellent nurses end up leaving and the hospital is left with the average ones.

If the physician chooses the nurse, the hospital will know which ones are good, and if no physician chooses a particular nurse, then they will realize she needs help. The issue is straightforward. Now, I know that nurses do not work every day. Therefore, every physician will choose a pool of five nurses, and his or her patients will be cared for by one of them only. The onus, of course, will be placed on nurses that can take care of patients because they are liked by many physicians.

All of a sudden, the weak nurse will work hard to get patients because otherwise will not get the hours or the bonuses, and this will work better than a million meetings and trainings because the nurse will be self-motivated. This is the same as for the physician: if he or she is inferior, he or she will not get the patients, and this will motivate the physician to be better. Fair and square. The physician has to do the same to get the referral ... Right?

Where Are We Going?

This is not an attack on the administrators and nurses. I know it sounds that way, but in reality, I wanted to underline that it is time that either administrators have the same responsibility and supervision as a physician, or that physicians take a step and become administrators and CEOs. I know that physicians are terrible with money, but I also know that some have a good head on their shoulders and will do a good job. A physician will ensure better peer review and a better understanding of the problems that physicians and nurses have.

A lot of nurses are in administration, but few nurses are evaluated by physicians, which actually would help to elevate their level of competency.

At the bottom line, just as the patient is a customer, physicians too are customers, essential customers. Think about the restaurant business. The chef makes the restaurant excellent or bad. Think about the physician as a chef and patients as restaurant customers. Would you not agree that our patients deserve the best meal, the best physician standard of care?

In this arena of fear and overcontrol, something needs to be changed. The dictatorial system will not last, and if it does, it will bring the hospital and quality down.

Only a strict collaboration between the administration and physicians will get the results. Utopia? Maybe it is.

We are in a different business—we are in the market of taking care of human beings so we need to talk straight and push dirt on each other.

Maybe administrators should observe and learn from the physicians' morbidity and mortality meetings where, at times, the presenter is mortified by the comments of his or her colleagues, but we all know that it is for the benefit of future patients, nothing personal.

Regulate Administrators in Healthcare

Sometimes you have to work in a hospital where your boss is "green" and has no understanding of what doctors and nurses or healthcare providers do. No background, no gray hair. Bad combination. Administrator leadership is not regulated; they do not have to provide continuing medical education. An MBA or MHA is good enough!

They do not respond to peer review, they do not have to go through 90 days of pain to apply for privileges in a hospital where your background is checked as well as your records and your capabilities, and if you do not treat enough patients, you don't get specific privileges. They should have rules and regulations for which they are responsible as the physician does.

Just as everybody wants physicians to provide the best quality care for the patients, we want the administrator to provide the best quality care to the hospital's employees, from doctors to nurses.

It is time that medical school trains not only the doctors of the future but also the administrators of the future. It's time that the administrators come not only with an MBA, as many physicians have an MBA as well, but also with specific training and a rotation in healthcare.

An excellent administrator should work in the hospital at the side of the physician during the day and at night, and feel the same frustration that we do when we receive an inappropriate call, and see the effect of this. They should have a rotation as the medical students do.

Furthermore, an administrator should have a rotation in nursing to understand the challenge that it sometimes is to be a nurse in a hospital where you have no support, and where you have to be the nurse, secretary, phlebotomist, etc.

As physicians, we should expect healthcare administrators to undergo much more rigorous training. First, if they come from manufacturing, they should do an internship in medical specialties to realize what they are getting into.

The administrator also needs to show this or her competency. As physicians takes exams, CME, and undergo peer review, the administrator should do the same.

An appropriate ad hoc committee should be formed with a physician present to grade the administrators of the hospital.

The profession of CEO, COO, and CFO of the hospital, and of the regional and national service, should be regulated as the physician is regulated.

It is not right that a CEO that messes up a hospital can resign and find a job in 2 weeks without any side effect. A physician in the same situation might be reported to his or her board or the state, and when he or she reapplies for a job, it might take 90 days to check references, performance, and achievements.

If the corporation asks the physician to improve his or her quality, I think it is fair that the physician asks the administrator to prove his or her quality daily, and by peer and board review as the physician does every day.

We suggest, therefore, that administrators have a board that regulates them, that they undergo regular exams and continuous education of about 30 hours a year and more scrutiny before they are given the chance to run a hospital and ruin all the healthcare workers that are involved in that.

How can you be a general if you have never been a soldier?

Notes

1. Verner S. Waite. Sham Peer Review: Napoleonic Law in Medicine. *Journal of American Physicians and Surgeons*, 8(3): 83–86, 2003.
2. The Cost of Courage: Complete Series. *The Pittsburgh Post-Gazette*. Available at: http://www.post-gazette.com/news/nation/2003/10/26/The-Cost-of-Courage-Complete-series/stories/200310260060.

Suggested Reading

1. Quizlet. HIM 465 Final Exam Chapter 9 Flashcards. Available at: https://quizlet.com/61385123/him-465-final-exam-chapter-9-flash-cards/.

Chapter 21

Big Pharma

Unspoken Issues

I was watching Trevor Noah's *The Daily Show* where he was talking about the influence of Big Pharma in the United States. He was focusing on a metric: Big Pharma pays $207 million a year in ... compared with 10.7 million from the weapon factories!

This is real and astonishing. Usually, we limit discussions on pharmaceutical companies to focus on physicians accepting gifts from Big Pharma, with nothing on the influence of Big Pharma on healthcare politics and the "gifts" in Washington.

It is interesting to see that, for England, they were pointing out the influence of pharmaceutical companies on the government, on the health department, on practitioners, politicians, etc. In the United States, the campaign against Big Pharma focused exclusively on the doctor. *Fortune* magazine reported in 2008 that the pharmaceutical industry was in the top three most profitable sectors in the United States, and that it had been like that for the past two decades.[1] It is a lucrative industry that utilizes different strategies to gain revenue. What is the process from developing to marketing drugs?

After FDA approval,[1] drugs have a patent that can last up to twenty years. This allows companies to keep exclusive rights to these brand-name drugs. It is only after this patent expires that other drug companies can use the formula to manufacture generic drugs. This allows the drugs to be bought at a significantly discounted rate in comparison with the brand-name drugs. A company makes the majority of its profit while it owns a drug patent. Money and time are invested in marketing this medication from many different angles, and a percentage of a company's budget is allocated to this because this strategy works. A pharmaceutical company, in a given year, will award more than a billion dollars to the marketing of medication. This is distributed in different directions, including direct marketing to the consumer and television and magazines adverts to inform people of the most recent drugs. Education awareness is a tool to market drugs. This empowers people to take responsibility for their health. Between 1991 and 2003, spending on direct advertisement in the United States increased 58 fold to $3.2 billion a year. This has led to more than a third of patients asking their healthcare providers about medications they have seen in the media and, as a result, when the patient asks for a drug by the name, he or she is more likely to receive a prescription for it from the healthcare provider. This shows that pharmaceutical company advertisements influence the consumer.

Relationship with Physicians and Hospitals

Pharmaceutical companies also employ representatives to visit care practitioners in the hospital and try to "educate and show the product." This also creates an influence directly on the health practitioner. There has been some controversy about whether the healthcare provider is having periodic contact with the pharmaceutical company's representative. Every year, more than $11 billion is spent on drug marketing, with half of the budget funding representative work.[1] It is essential to identify the extent of this relationship and its ultimate impact. Food, friendship, and flattery are all powerful tools for persuasion, particularly when they are combined.

This was part of the finding of the attorney general and consumer education grant program in 2004. This was secondary to the Warner-Lambert settlement related to an allegation of an unlawful marketing campaign. Pharmaceutical companies can also collect information about prescriptions in counties, towns, etc., and the orders filled in a given community. Pharmacies produce these records and, after taking out the patient's name, they sell these records to pharmaceutical companies for the right amount of money. The pharmaceutical companies buy this information to monitor the market. They can see how many of these practitioners they contact, how many prescribe their drugs, and how easy it is to influence physicians. Also, another way to control prescribing is by giving samples to the physicians. Therefore, the sample is given to the patient for free, and the patient then gets used to that medication and is going to ask for or buy the same medicine. Companies have been giving a lot of gifts to physicians, but not only to physicians. Gifts have been given to physicians, but there was more than a gift given to the healthcare facility, the hospital, and politicians, which was never shown in the investigation. All campaigns against contributions from pharmaceutical companies to healthcare providers have focused on the physicians and the nurse practitioners only. They never focus on the big healthcare facilities or politicians. For the physician, there were minimal items like pens and pads, books, and food. Meals, trips, and presentations have also been included. Pharmaceutical companies have been shown to influence residents and physicians differently using meals and travel. The point of concern arose when representatives prioritized the promotion of the product more than the patient's welfare, which is unethical. Roughly 90% of physicians interact with pharmaceutical representatives, and some have a preference toward certain medications over others. There have been some steps taken to combat this tactic. In July 2006, the American Medical Association (AMA) established the prescription data restriction program, which gave physicians the right to withhold prescription details from pharmaceutical representatives and their supervisors. The pharmaceutical industry has been using money to influence not only prescribing practitioners but also in teaching and research. Big Pharma has responded by revising its code and, on January 1, 2009, reaffirming that interactions between pharmaceutical company representatives and healthcare professionals should be focused on informing the healthcare professional about the product and providing scientific education information only.

Big Pharma, Medical School, and Administrators

Pharmaceutical companies have been focusing on targeting medical schools, and a policy has therefore been made to restrict the influence of Big Pharma in medical schools. It is true that pharmaceutical companies invest a tremendous amount of money in research, development, and marketing. It is through marketing that healthcare providers and patients can be influenced into prescribing or requesting specific medication. Whether deliberate or not, Big Pharma develop a type of misunderstanding that might represent innocent business practice. So, out of respect for healthcare driven by financial gain and boundaries must be set at all levels when the welfare of the patient and professional is at stake. But what are the stakes? An article by Michelle Llamas[2] looked at how the critics contended that Big Pharma used manipulative tactics and expensive advertisements to sway lawmakers, the FDA, and the public to increase sales. The public are exposed to misleading promotions and publicity. Many examples of this were presented in the article. For example, selling testosterone to men was a common practice, but no warning had been placed on the label that testosterone given to men can lead to heart problems until the FDA added this warning after a million men had already been exposed to that risk. Doctors, scientists, research organizations, medical journals, teaching hospitals, universities, and medical schools have all exhibited a disturbing conflict of interest with respect to Big Pharma. In this article, said the author stated that private charities and foundations accounted for a mere 5% of the estimated $100 billion spent on biomedical research in the U.S. each year, while pharmaceutical and medical device companies contributed approximately 60%.[3]

Also of interest in this article, Michelle Llamas showed that the trade group Pharma included several current and former staff members who had previously served in the political arena. This included:

- 36 people who worked for members of Congress
- 13 who worked for a federal agency
- 12 who work for the congressional committee
- Two who worked for the White House
- One who worked for the "system"

These are the people who help Big Pharma to be competitive and to have a connection at their level.

Why Do We Pay More for Medication?

Why do Americans pay more than any other country for medication? Americans spend more than any other country in the world for pharmaceuticals—in some cases, thousands of dollars more for prescriptions.[4] Big Pharma says that this occurs because of the astronomical cost of developing new drugs, but I disagree with that. I noticed, when going around the world giving speeches, that there was a device for controlling obesity which would sell in the United States for $3500. You could buy the same device in Mexico for $1500 and in China for $1000. So the question is why this device cost $2000 more in the United States compared with South America and $2500 more compared with Asia. The company was the same, therefore the cost of developing the new drug was the same. The new system was not a good excuse because the price varied in different countries. I noticed the same thing when traveling in different countries, whereby the cost of a regular anti-fever medication was astronomically high in the United States while the same medicine in a different country was less than half the price.

Going back to the article by Michelle Llamas, as cost fact analysis was included. The United States allows drug companies to set the price for drugs and protects them from free market competition. Other countries limit what a company can charge based on the benefit of the drug. The real cost of developing a pill is shrouded in mystery, with many unverifiable figures reported by Big Pharma. While a company claims that each new drug costs $1.2 billion, the actual cost is $60 million. The industry also avoids talking about how much it spends on marketing, which is almost double what they pay for research. In the same article, Llamas reports that the significant amount of cash Big Pharma bestows on government and regulatory bodies is small when compared with the millions spent each year on direct consumer advertising. Joanna James,[5] in her article, reported that the U.S. is one of the only countries in the world whose government allows prescription drugs to be advertised on T.V. (the other is New Zealand). In 2015, Big Pharma spent $5.4 billion on direct consumer advertising and fired off about eighty ads an hour according to Nielson. Big Pharma also employs doctors, researchers, and institutions. The industry persuades doctors to allow ghostwriting, paying physicians to attach their names to definitive articles about a particular drug with the goal of seeing it published in a reputable medical journal. Often the comments are a little more than advertisement written by a company, with paid copywriters showcasing a new product. Big Pharma uses ghostwriters to promote more new drugs including anti-depressants, multiple drugs. Furthermore, even when a medical reviewer writes a complete reassessment of a new drug for a medical journal, it is common practice for those supposedly unbiased professionals to be on the Big Pharma payroll.

The UK

The UK is the third largest direct exporter of pharmaceuticals. Nevertheless, healthcare in the UK deserves considerable praise for its open criticism of the UK government and the European market, both of which are starting to believe that the trade imperative and priorities are inseparable. George Freeman MP[6] wrote a report explicitly mentioning some anti-depressant and anti-inflammatory medication that created side effects, but nobody had looked into that, and the medicines were placed on the market regardless. The committee showed that some drugs created more disease, and that 3%–5% of all hospital admissions in the UK, per year, were secondary to adverse drug reactions, accounting for costs of £500 million per year. This produced almost £750 million per year at that point, when the pound was robust. The report shows that ghostwriters are used to make drugs more marketable or to find words to describe the same things and the same side effects without saying what is actually happening. Isn't that the life of the government nowadays, or the company that talks about a proper word without understanding the words that they say? It is interesting that the report shows that ghostwriters, in conjunction with the suppression of negative trial results, are harmful. If doctors do not have access to fair and accurate accounts of clinical trials, then they cannot be expected to make informed decisions when deciding how best to treat their patient. The committee found a lot of breach of communication when the side effects came, and therefore they suggest a higher regulatory system for this. Now, at the end of the report, they find that the pharmaceutical company was to blame for providing hospitality to doctors and for paying what are sometimes significant sums of money to key opinion leaders. A medical practitioner, if evaluating a drug, can be influenced by payment and by other things. Some are affiliated with the company, some are sponsors of clinical trials, and some are using the medication and might not always be fair in their evaluation of the medication. This report[6] finishes by describing the government's involvement:

> The fundamental weakness in a government is dealing with the phar-
> maceutical industry, namely the Department of Health plays a role in
> promoting health and acting as a sponsor of the industry. These roles,
> as committee states in the report, have not proved compatible. Health
> and trade priorities are not always identical. In their combination, it

leads to a lack of clarity, focus, and commitment to help the outcomes. The report concludes that the secretary of the state for health will put patients' priority first. As a result, the committee recommended that responsibility represented interest of the pharmaceutical industry should move into the department of trade industry and not to the health department.

What this is saying is that healthcare departments should not be directly connected to the industry in a way that it can become biased by the industry.

A Classical Recent Example

The last example of this saga is the case of Martin Shkreli, known as 'Pharma Bro,' who was the most hated man in the U.S. in 2015 when he decided to increase the cost of an important medication for HIV treatment from $13.50 to $750, an increase of 5000%. Shkreli had his own hedge funds (MSMB Capital Management, and MSMB Healthcare) and at 34 bought the pharma company Turing Pharmaceuticals. He was finally placed in jail for seven years, and fined $75,000, which is peanuts compared with what he made hurting patients. The company's name was Retrophin, and it was quoted on Nasdaq. The same Nasdaq threw him out after realizing in 2014 that he was using company money for personal use. He also had to return $7.4 million in losses.

I wonder how many patients suffered or died all these years because of this greedy person, and why they could not buy the drug outside of the US?

Notes

1. James Rhee. The Influence of the Pharmaceutical Industry on Healthcare Practitioners' Prescribing Habits. *The Internet Journal of Academic Physician Assistants* 7(1): 1–7, 2008.
2. Michelle Llamas. Selling Side Effects: Big Pharma's Marketing Machine. *NCHR*. 2016. Available at: http://www.center4research.org/selling-side-effects-big-pharmas-marketing-machine/.
3. Kristin Compton. Big Pharma and Medical Device Manufacturers. *DrugWatch*. 2018. Available at: https://www.drugwatch.com/manufacturers/.
4. Steve Blum. 2013, August 6. Comcast Loves Publicly Subsidized Overbuilds, When it's Doing the Building. *TellusVenture*. Available at: https://www.tellusventure.com/blog/comcast-loves-publicly-subsidised-overbuilds-when-its-doing-the-building/.
5. Colette Greenstein. 2017, October 5. Joanna James' *A Fine Line* Doc Screens at GlobeDocs Film Festival. *Bay State Banner*. p. 19.
6. Tom Robinson. 2014, December 1. George Freeman: UK Pharma is Vital for Our Landscape. *Pharmafile*. Available at: http://www.pharmafile.com/news/195905/george-freeman-uk-pharma-vital-our-landscape.

Suggested Reading

1. Money-Fortune 500 Magazine. FORTUNE 500: Our annual ranking of America's largest corporations-Top Industries: Most profitable. 2008. Available at: http://money.cnn.com/magazines/fortune/fortune500/2008/performers/industries/profits/ (accessed January 24, 2009).

2. Alison J. Huang. The Rise of Direct-to-Consumer Advertising of Prescription Drugs in the United States. *Journal of the American Medical Association* 284: 2240, 2000.

3. Steven P. Drug Representatives: Giving You Lunch or Stealing Your Soul? *Dermatology Online Journal* 13: 1–6, 2007.

4. PhRMA. PhRMA Statement on Restricting Drug Marketing and Education. February 13, 2007. Available at: http://www.phrma.org/news_room/press_releases/phrma_statement_on_restricting_drug_marketing_and_education/ (accessed April 3, 2008).

5. Marcia Angell. *The Truth about the Drug Companies: How They Deceive Us and What to Do about It.* New York, NY: Random House, 2005.

6. Donald L. Barlett and James B. Steele. *Critical Condition: How Healthcare in America became Big Business-and Bad Medicine.* New York, NY: Random House, 2006.

7. Susan Chimonas, Troyen A. Brennan and David J. Rothman. Physician and Drug Representatives: Exploring the Dynamics of the Relationship. *Journal of General Internal Medicine* 22: 184–190, 2007.

8. John Abramson. *Overdosed America: The Broken Promise of American Medicine.* New York, NY: Harper Collins, 2008.

9. Ashley Wazana. Physicians, and the Pharmaceutical Industry: Is a Gift Ever Just a Gift? *Journal of the American Medical Association* 283: 373–380, 2000.

10. Ray Moynihan. Who Pays for the Pizza? Redefining the Relationships Between Doctors and Drug Companies. 1: Entanglement. *British Medical Journal* 31(326): 1189–1192, 2003.

11. Adriane Fugh-Berman and Shahram Ahari. Following the Script: How Drug Reps Make Friends and Influence Doctors. *PLOS Medicine* 4: 621–625, 2007.

12. Nick Freemantle, Richard Johnson, Jane Dennis, Andrew Kennedy, and Mike Marchment. Sleeping with the Enemy? A Randomized Controlled Trial of a Collaborative Health Authority/Industry intervention to Influence Prescribing Practice. *British Journal of Clinical Pharmacology* 49: 174–179, 2000.

13. Peter Doshi. From Promises to Policies: Is Big Pharma Delivering on Transparency? *BMJ*, 348. 2014.

14. Molly Scott Cato. 2014, April 23. The Real Reason Drugs Cost So Much – And Why Big Pharma is So Rich. *The Guardian.* Available at: https://www.theguardian.com/commentisfree/2014/apr/23/reason-drugs-cost-so-much-big-pharmaceuticals-rich.

MEDICARE AND MEDICAID

Chapter 22

The Future of the Entitlement Program

Medicare Part A and B

The Health Insurance for the Aged and Disabled Act (title XVIII of the Social Security Act), known as "Medicare," was built in favor of Americans aged 65 years and above. This is a program of health insurance designed to assist the nation's elderly in meeting hospital, medical, and other healthcare costs. Health insurance coverage has also been extended to patients under 65 qualifying as disabled and those having end-stage renal disease (ESRD) or Lou Gehrig's disease. The program includes two related health insurance programs—hospital insurance (HI) (Part A) and supplementary medical insurance (SMI) (Part B).[1]

Benefit for beneficiaries covered by Part A provides for treatment after hospitalization. The purpose of this is to find more economical alternatives to inpatient care.

Payments for services rendered to beneficiaries by hospitals, SNFs, and home health agencies are sent to the provider. In each benefit period, payment may be made for up to 90 inpatient hospital days, and 100 days of post-hospital extended care services. Hospices also provide Part A hospital insurance services such as short-term inpatient care. Under Part A, patients are eligible to elect for hospice care under Medicare, although an individual must be entitled to Part A of Medicare and be certified as being terminally ill. An individual is considered to be terminally ill if he or she has a medical prognosis that his or her life expectancy is six months or less if the illness runs its ordinary course.[2]

Part A is financed through separate payroll contributions paid by employees, employers, and self-employed persons.[1]

Part B is financed by the monthly premiums of those who voluntarily enroll in the program and by the Federal Government, which makes contributions from general revenues.[2]

What is the Entitlement Program?

Since the mid-1980s, entitlement programs have accounted for more than half of all federal spending. Unfortunately, this can produce uncontrollable expenses as interest payments on the national debt and the payment obligations arising from long-term contracts already entered into by the government in previous years. Entitlement programs leave Congress with no more than about 25% of the annual budget to be scrutinized for possible cutbacks through the regular appropriations process. This very substantially reduces the practicality of trying to counteract the ups and downs of the overall economy through a "discretionary" fiscal policy because so very little of the budget is available for significant alteration by the Appropriations and Budget committees on short notice.[3]

The federal government and the states currently jointly fund Medicaid. Medicaid provides health coverage to millions of Americans, including the elderly, low-income adults, children, and people with disabilities. The most recent suggestion by the government was to convert Medicaid into a block grant program for states, and then to cap the grants. But historical data on grants indicate that, over time, this will result in a decline in Medicaid funding, and the nation's neediest citizens will feel the impact.[4]

Funding with Tax Cuts

Republicans passed a nearly $1.5 trillion tax cut, which the Congressional Budget Office said would trigger sequestration across some significant mandatory spending programs, like Medicare, federal student loans, and agriculture subsidies, and even some funding for customs and border patrols. This waiver would allow Congress to bypass the sequestration law meant to keep the deficit in check.

Republicans, who have long under-evaluated the dangers of the national debt, have come under fire recently for pushing a deficit-busting tax cut that's primarily geared toward corporations and America's highest earners.[5]

By interpreting the Republican tax bill, we can summarize the following:

1. First, the triggering of mandatory spending programs by a tax bill should be avoided since it is not safe at present to make budget cuts.
2. By the most recent estimates, the bill will increase the deficit by $1.46 trillion in the first ten years, or—when adjusted for economic growth—by $1 trillion.

3. Already, there have been reports that the actual cost of the tax bill could even be higher; upward of $2 trillion when considering the likely renewal of temporary individual tax cuts.
4. Medicaid, Social Security, food stamps, and all social safety net programs are exempt from this tax cut. Medicare, social services, grants, student loans, and mandatory spending in the Affordable Care Act (other than Medicaid expansion) could instead be part of the cut.
5. Cuts to Medicare are capped at 4%, about $25 billion per year, meaning cuts to the other mandatory spending programs would have to make up the difference.[5]

Where Are the Entitlement Programs Going?

As Congress works to reconcile their so-called tax reform legislation, few economists agree that the tax bill is merely a gift to wealthy donors who threatened to cut off their donations to the party unless taxes are cut.

With even more massive deficit spending as a result of the tax cuts, the government has to turn its attention to reducing federal expenditures. The most significant drivers of federal spending are Social Security, Medicare, Medicaid, military spending, and interest on the debt. Defense and interest payments will not be cut. That leaves the entitlement programs standing alone.[4] Cutting the entitlement program seems to be the only logical solution to recover the loss of money from the tax cut funds.

Starving the Beast

According to the *Huffington Post*,[4]

> "Starving the beast" is a political strategy conservatives developed decades ago for reducing government spending. In 1978, economist and future Fed Chairman Alan Greenspan told a congressional committee, "Let us remember that the basic purpose of any tax cut program in today's environment is to reduce the momentum of expenditure growth by restraining the amount of revenue available and trust that there is a political limit to deficit spending." Liberal economist Paul Krugman later observed, "Rather than proposing unpopular spending cuts, Republicans would push through popular tax cuts, with the deliberate intention of worsening the government's fiscal position. Spending cuts could be sold as a necessity rather than a choice." It seems the history is repeating nowadays again.

Notes

1. Medicare Hospital Manual Health Care Financing. Available at: https://www.cms.gov/Regulations-and-Guidance/Guidance/Transmittals/downloads/R75SOMA.pdf.
2. Medicare General Information, Eligibility, And Entitlement. Available at: https://www.cms.gov/regulations-and-guidance/guidance/manuals/downloads/ge101c01.pdf.
3. Entitlement Program: A Glossary Of Political Economy Terms. Available at: https://www.auburn.edu/~johnspm/gloss/entitlement_program.
4. Joe Peyronnin. 2017, December 8. The GOP Targets Entitlements. *Huffington Post*. Available at: https://www.huffingtonpost.com/entry/the-gop-targets-entitlements_us_5a2ad328e4b04e0bc8f3b43c.
5. Tara Golshan. 2017, December 21. Republicans are Preventing Their Tax Bill From Triggering a $25 Billion Cut to Medicare. *Vox*. Available at: https://www.vox.com/policy-and-politics/2017/11/14/16651184/gop-tax-bill-medicare-cut-paygo.

Chapter 23

Disproportionate Medicaid Funding

Medicaid State Payments

Medicaid State Plans Determine State Payment Methodology for Medicaid Services

States must ensure that they can fund their share of Medicaid expenditures for the care and services available under their state plan. Recognized sources of funding for the state share of Medicaid payments include

- Legislative appropriations to the single state agency
- Inter-governmental transfers (IGTs)
- Certified public expenditures (CPEs)
- Permissible taxes and provider donations

Before the Centers for Medicare and Medicaid Services (CMS) approves a state plan amendment, it must verify that state funding sources meet statutory and regulatory requirements so that it can authorize federal financial participation (FFP) for the covered services.

Medicaid Spending

Medicaid receives $1 out of every $6 spent on healthcare in the United States. Therefore, the states and the federal government provide a significant source of funding for the program. Medicaid has been expanded under the Affordable Care Act (ACA), and in the Obamacare era, more people applied to Medicaid. The financial model of Medicaid has remained unchanged since it was established. The program guarantees to match state/federal expenditure and therefore allows federal funding into a state budget based on actual costs and needs. Federal funding is going toward children's health insurance programs (CHIP), which will be extended until 2019. These programs will be available for primary care, preventive care, community-based long-term services support, and other programs). The federal government pays the state a per-program expenditure called Federal Medical Assistance Percentage (FMAP). This varies by county, by ProCapita, and by year. State funding can range from between 50% and 75% to a maximum of 82%. This FMAP is adjusted every 3-year cycle between the federal government and the state. The state provides direct service, and has its rates, and each state can offer a different standard of cost provision for service, reviews the different markets, and adjusts the percentage that Medicaid pays per the Medicare rate. Providers are paid under monthly capitation pay rates (the physician). A state plan amendment (SPA) needs to be provided by the state to the CMS for review approval before a change to the pay terminology can be applied in a different state. Therefore, Medicaid plays a role in federal government and the state budget. This is a program that is budgeted and is now ranked third in the country after Medicare and Social Security. It is both an expenditure and a source of federal revenue in a state budget. The state needs to agree and balance its budget to collect tax from the federal government and to pay out according to each state's needs and necessities. The difference between Medicaid and Medicare is that Medicare is social insurance, that is, a health insurance program for patients older than 65. Medicaid, however, is funded only by the federal government, and the money flows into the state. This is a program for social protection and social insurance. In 2014, the implementation of major ACA coverage expansions required an increase in funding for Medicaid because more people were applying for insurance.

Under fee-for-service arrangements, states pay providers directly for services. States may develop their payment rates based on:

- The costs of providing the service
- A review of what commercial payers pay in the private market
- A percentage of what Medicare pays for equivalent services

Under managed care arrangements, states contract with organizations to deliver care through networks and pay providers. Approximately 70% of Medicaid enrollees are served through managed care delivery systems, where providers are paid on a monthly capitation payment rate.

Macro-Economy and Medicaid

Because Medicaid is funded by the federal government, the national micro-economy is directly connected with Medicaid funding. In the past 15 years, for instance, there were substantial changes in Medicaid enrollment. One was in 2001 and one in 2009, during the two major recessions of the past two decades. With the economic downturn, there was increased demand for this program, and state tax revenue was therefore negatively affected. This placed more pressure on the state budget, and increased federal assistance was therefore requested, not just at the Medicaid level but also for tax revenue. Congress passed an FMAP rate to help support states during the recession. This was done in 2009 as a part of the American Recovery and Reinvestment Act (ARRA). The ARRA matched rates provided to states by over $100 billion in addition to federal funding over two years. Once the federal dollars from the Medicaid program feed into the state's economy, the state's economy improves. This affects the state's budget, which increases, but spending on Medicare is expected to grow but with matching funds down to 90% in 2020 and remain thereafter and therefore a search on federal funding is going to be required by 2020, although the federal government does not have the funds necessary to support Medicaid. The states are always going to struggle to match the expenditure; as economic conditions improve, spending grows and tax revenue increases, and this will balance the budget of the state. It is not as easy as we think.

Crash Funding

Everybody is talking about crash funding, but its correct name is disproportionate share hospital payments (DSH). DSH is a source of finance available to hospitals that serve Medicaid and low-income insurance patients. In many states, this payment has been crucial to the financial stability and safety net of the hospital. With an increased number of patients applying for Medicaid under the ACA, the law and the federal government have been calling for the increased allocation of money for DSH with the new ACA, and the more people that apply, the more the state can expect an increase in uncompensated care that the hospital must provide. Therefore, more federal government money is needed. The state has some flexibility in determining the source of funding for a non-federal share of Medicaid spending. The primary source of funding comes from the state general fund appropriation. Over the past decade, state use of other funds has increased slightly but steadily, but relies primarily on taxes and fees to finance the state share of Medicaid. In 2013, the federal DSH payment was $16.4 billion; the state can determine which hospitals receive which level of DSH payment at their discretion, but the process has two caps: one at the state level and one at the facility level. The state level cap is in place is because each state has an amount of money (cap) that it can use for paying the hospital. This is usually calculated from the expenditure of the previous year. At the facility level, Medicaid DSH is limited to 100% of costs incurred for serving Medicaid and uninsured patients that are not compensated by Medicaid. Therefore, based on the assumption that there are going to be more patients that require this type of care because more have applied for Obamacare and Medicaid, there are going to be more hospitals and more assistance needed for DSH funding and for this vision. Unfortunately, the federal government has called for a decrease in state DSH funding. It looks like there is going to be a reduction of $2 million in 2018.

Suggested Reading

1. Medicare Budget and Performance. Available at: https://www.cms.gov/About-CMS/Agency-Information/PerformanceBudget/index.html.
2. Mark V. Pauly. Should We be Worried about High Real Medical Spending Growth in the United States? *Health Affairs* [Web Exclusive], W3: 15–27, 2003.
3. Stephen Heffler, Sheila Smith, Sean Keehan, M. Kent Clemens, Mark Zezza and Christopher Truffer. Health Spending Projections Through 2013. *Health Affairs* [Web Exclusive], W4: 79–93, 2004.
4. L. Lorenzoni, A. Belloni and F. Sassi. Health Care Expenditure and Health Policy in the USA versus other High-Spending OECD Countries. *The Lancet* 384(9937): 83–92, 2014.
5. John Holahan and Stacey McMorrow. Medicare and Medicaid Spending trends and the deficit debates. *New England Journal of Medicine* 367: 393–395, 2012.
6. V. de Rugy. Facts on Medicare Spending and Finances. Available at: http://kff.org/medicare/fact-sheet/medicare-spending-and-financing-fact-sheet/.
7. T. Foertsch and J. Antos. The Economic and Fiscal Effects of Financing Medicare's Unfunded Liabilities. October 11, 2005.
8. Safety Net Pool Care Program. Available at: http://federalsafetynet.com/safety-net-programs.html
9. Healthcare Safety Net Resources. Available at: http://federalsafetynet.com/safety-net-programs.html.
10. Medicaid Disproportionate Share Hospital (DSH) Payments. Available at: https://www.medicaid.gov/medicaid/financing-and-reimbursement/dsh/index.html.
11. Federal Medicaid Disproportionate Share Hospital (DSH) Payments. Available at: http://kff.org/medicaid/state-indicator/federal-dsh-allotments/?currentTimeframe=0&sortModel=%7B%22colId%22:%22Location%22,%22sort%22:%22asc%22%7D.
12. Disproportionate Share Hospital (DSH). The Medicare DSH Adjustment (42 CFR 412.106). Available at: https://www.cms.gov/Medicare/Medicare-Fee-for-Service-Payment/AcuteInpatientPPS/dsh.html.
13. Who is Paying for Medicaid? Available at: https://www.medicare.gov/your-medicare-costs/help-paying-costs/medicaid/medicaid.html.
14. How is Medicare Funded? Available at: https://www.medicare.gov/about-us/how-medicare-is-funded/medicare-funding.html.
15. How does Medicaid Work? Available at: http://people.howstuffworks.com/how-Medicaid-works4.htm.
16. What are Medicare and Medicaid? *Medical News Today*. Available at: http://www.medicalnewstoday.com/info/medicare-medicaid.
17. Anne B. Martin, Lekha Whittle, Stephen Heffler, Mary Carol Barron, Andrea Sisko, and Benjamin Washington. Health Spending By State Of Residence, 1991–2004. *Health Affairs*, 26(6): 25 Years in the Health Sphere.

Chapter 24

Medicare and Medicaid: Unifying or Crushing? A Financial Nightmare

Healthcare Expenditure

The healthcare system is always at the center of attention for its expenditure. The increase in medical spending by the United States is unmatched in other developed countries, as evidenced by OECD analyses.[1,2]

Here are some example of the expenditure. In 2013, Medicare spending grew 3.4% to about 585.7 billion, or 20% of total net health expenses, while Medicaid grew 6.1% to 449.4 billion. or 15% of total net health expenses.[3-6]. Private health insurance spending grew 2.8% to 961.7 billion, or 33% of total expenses.[7] Hospital spending grew 5.6% to 1,036.1 billion in 2015, greater than the 4.6% it grew in 2014. In 2015, the National Health Expenditure (NHE),[8,9] grew 5.8% to 3.2 trillion, about $9,990,000 per person, and accounted for 17.8% of the gross domestic product (GDP).[10,11] Medicare spending grew 4.5% to 646.2 billion, 20% of the total NHE. Medicaid spending grew 9.7% to 545.1 billion in 2015, or 70% of the total NHE; private health insurance grew 7.2% to 1,072.1 billion, compared with 33% of the total NHE; and out-of-pocket spending grew 2.6% to 338.1 billion in 2015, compared with 11% of total NHE. Physician and clinical surveys expenditure grew 6.3% to 634.9 billion, compared with 4.8% in 2014.[8,12,13] Prescription drug spending increased 9% to 324.6 billion, compared with 12.4% in 2014.[13,14] The federal government, therefore, supported the largest share of total health expenditure, 20.7%, with household expenditure at 27.7%. The private business share of spending accounted for 19.9%.[10,12,15]

These increases, while disturbing, cannot be interpreted in and of themselves because the spending increments depend upon inflation, the overall status of the economy, and the growth of the population.[16–18]

In this chapter, we evaluate the expenses of Medicare and Medicaid between 1966 and 2015 and calculate the annual percentage of total healthcare expenditures represented by insurance expenditures, including CMS (Medicare, Medicaid, CHIP) and hospital and physician/clinical expenditures. The goal is to find out if the CMS is well funded and, with the baby boomer generation increasingly pocketing Medicare funding, if the system will be valuable and sustainable in the future.

We are going to evaluate the numbers and the information released by the CMS Centers for Medicare & Medicaid Services[19] to assess the expenditure and, based on this, see if federal and private insurance match while checking for simulations and divergences.

How can we look at this matter in perspective? We analyzed healthcare expenditure over time to identify the problems with the hope of enabling policymakers to understand where the programs are going and if there is a possibility to unify the two plans and make them one.

Evaluation of CMS Data

The source of information was the Centers for Medicare & Medicaid Services.[19] We used the NHE2015 table to analyze the data. Joinpoint regression (Joinpoint Program 4.4.0.0[20]) was used to produce estimates and standard errors of annual changes in percent (ACP) and joined points (years in which ACP changed) using a linear equation and the grid search method, permitting the data itself to correct for autocorrelation. The 1966–2015 annual percent of total healthcare expenditure was evaluated and compared, and represented as (1) out of pocket and insurance expenditures; (2) private insurance and CMS (Medicare, Medicaid, CHIP); (3) Medicare and Medicaid expenditures, 1966–2015; and (4) hospital and physician/clinical expenditure.

Reading the Data

Figure 24.1 displays the annual percentages of total medical expenses by category, estimated join points (black dots), and yearly changes in percent (ACP, slopes of line segments). Where the 95% confidence interval (CI) of the ACP excludes 0, a ^ symbol is placed beside the value. The vertical line at 2010 demarcates the adoption of the Affordable Care Act (ACA).

The upper left figure shows decreasing out-of-pocket and increasing health insurance expenditure, consistent with the generalized increase in the cost of healthcare

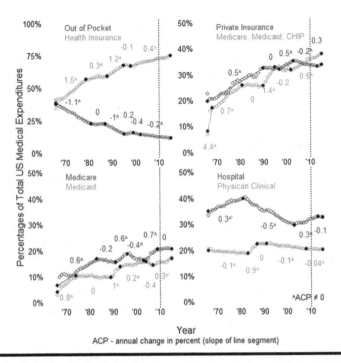

Figure 24.1 **Percentage of total US Medical expenses: Medicare, Medicaid, Hospitals, Physicians, Private Insurances and out of pocket from the 1970s to 2015.**

beyond that which individuals can afford. The upper right figure shows that whereas private health insurance expediture stopped increasing in 1990, CMS entities (Medicare, Medicaid, CHIP) continued to rise throughout the period; this is consistent with the notion that expenses began to rise above the affordability of private insurance in 1990. The bottom left figure shows rises in Medicare and Medicaid expenditure, with stabilization of the former since 2009. The bottom right graph shows divergent tendencies: for hospitals, the 1981–2003 decline reflects the adoption of diagnosis-related group savings, while the 2003–2013 rise may indicate the ability of hospitals to capitalize on their captive patient market concerning drugs as a result of the Medicare. Prescription drugs, improvements, and the Modernization Act expenses: for physicians and caregivers, apart from an increase and stabilization between 1983 and 1991, possibly reflecting an adjustment to the implementation of DRGs, there was a steady decline in the proportion of healthcare spending devoted to physicians and clinical care.

The final point should be emphasized, as the relatively recent adoption of nurse practitioners and physician assistants cannot be said to have influenced the proportion of healthcare spending that goes to clinicians; if anything, the change halved the annual rate of decline after 2008. Changes that can reasonably be said to have resulted from the adoption of the ACA included an increase in private insurance beginning in 2013. This was likely due to the increased affordability of insurance and a decrease in hospital care expenditure in 2013, possibly due to decreased visits to emergency rooms occasioned by an increase in the proportion of the population that was insured.

What to Expect from These Data

Although studies of healthcare costs over time are diverse and plentiful, this is likely the first to use joinpoint regression to analyze proportions of healthcare spending over time. Joinpoint regression analyses of proportions are valuable because they eliminate the need to adjust dollar figures for inflation, consider autocorrelation as part of the assessment, and permit generalized conclusions by percentages that cannot be made with them as the significant facility as with annual spending figures.[21,22] Perhaps most notable is the steady increase in the proportion of spending accounted for by CMS programs, which, if trends continue, will soon surpass 50% of all healthcare spending.[23–25] At such a time, the debate over single-payer healthcare will be moot as, for the most part, the US will then be a single payer state, no matter how private insurance is provisioned. The long-term effects of the ACA cannot be adjudged with certainty given the limited number of years in which it has been useful; the initial results, however, look promising.

Recessions have been noted[5,6,26–28] in 1969–1970, 1973–1975, 1980–1982, 1990–1992, 2001, and 2007–2009; the figure shows that no consistent effect can be discerned from recessions upon the different components of medical spending. Precisely because the changes in tax revenue are not reflected in changes in parts of medical expenditures, it is essential that states consider, when preparing budgets, the revenue shortfalls that will of necessity occur with respect to Medicaid and CHIP.[29,30]

From the perspective of the hospital and clinicians, besides the role provided the ACA, it does not retain its present effect of insurance for all. Medicare and Medicaid rose in generally similar terms while private insurance dropped, meaning that both hospitals and clinicians will increasingly see the government as the payer.[31] A difference between Medicaid and Medicare is that the former has catastrophic coverage while the latter does not. This means that the ability of hospitals and clinicians to recoup expenses associated with high-cost patients will be more favorable as respects Medicaid; currently, there exists a 62% rate increase for the hospital safety net associated with Medicaid.[32] A point of interest is the Safety Net Care Pool Program, which is part of the ACA; the benefits of this program are geared toward rural, not urban hospitals.[33,34]

Nurse practitioners and physician assistants cannot be said to have influenced the proportion of healthcare spending that goes to clinicians, as the expenditure for a nurse practitioner is similar to that of a physician for insurance purposes.

The effects of crash funding, called disproportionate share hospital payments (DSH), remain a source of interest. DSH assists hospitals with high levels of Medicaid and low-income insurance patients, often being a vital factor with respect to the financial stability of such hospitals.[35-37] Because the number of patients applying for Medicaid has increased under ACA,[18,38-41] the resources of hospitals— even with DHS—have been strained, likely requiring additional federal assistance in this respect. This difficulty, as shown by this study, will partly be mitigated if the ACA retains its current role, through the increased role of private insurance in the medical economy.

More data from up to 2017 came out while I was writing this chapter, but I stopped at 2015 because I had already shown:

1. The increase in expenditure over the past 20 years, with no need to check and additional two years more and that
2. That Medicare and Medicaid will eventually produce the same expenses, and that they are heading for a collision which can cause the healthcare system to crash once and for all if we do not do something substantial.

Possible Solutions

The ACA, although promising in respect to changing the declining role of private insurance in the medical economy, will likely not forestall the increase in government spending that is required. For this reason, a frank conversation regarding the role of government in healthcare is warranted. Similarities in the rise in Medicare and Medicaid spending argue for combining the two into a single program, with the addition of catastrophic insurance for all not currently covered by these two programs. The role of private health insurance in this respect would then be to provision non-catastrophic coverage for the working public. A solution to the funding problem associated with such a chance lies in updating the Medicare tax rate, which would cover this, to 4% on the first $200,000 and 6% above $200,000. With Medicaid and Medicare thus united, we would have more streamlined protocols and a stronger financial base.

Acknowledgment

Dr. Mitchel Wachtell, from Texas Tech. University, Lubbock, Texas, for co-authoring the original article with me and for performing the research and statistical analysis (Frezza, EE, Wachtel, M. Medicare and Medicaid: Unifying or Crushing? This is the Dilemma. *Public Health Open Access Journal*, 1(2): 109–115. Troy, MI: Medwin. 2017. Available at: https://medwinpublishers.com/PHOA/PHOA16000109.pdf.

Notes

1. OECD 2016 Healthcare Analysis. Available at: http://www.oecd.org/els/health-systems/health-data.htm.
2. US Healthcare from a Global Perspective. Available at: http://www.commonwealthfund.org/publications/issue-briefs/2015/oct/us-health-care-from-a-global-perspective.
3. The analysis assumes that payments rates increase at 1% per year from 2013 to 2035, and does not reflect the 0% update in the American Taxpayers Relief Act of 2012.
4. Richard Kronick and Rosa Po. 2013, January 7. Growth in Medicare Spending per Beneficiary Continues to Hit Historic Lows. ASPE. Available at: https://aspe.hhs.gov/basic-report/growth-medicare-spending-beneficiary-continues-hit-historic-lows.
5. Congressional Budget Office. Letter to the Honorable Nancy Pelosi, 2010. Available at: http://www.cbo.gov/system/files/cbofiles/ftpdocs/113xx/doc11379/a.
6. Center for Medicare and Medicaid Center. National Health Expenditure Data (fed government data). Available at: https://www.cms.gov/Research-Statistics-Data-and-Systems/Statistics-Trends-and-Reports/NationalHealthExpendData/index.html.
7. Congressional Budget Office. Medicare Baseline, March 9, 2015.
8. *2015 Annual Report of the Boards of Trustees of the Federal Hospital Insurance and Federal Supplementary Medical Insurance Trust Funds, July 22, 2015, Table V.B1.* Available at: https://www.cms.gov/Research-Statistics-Data-and-Systems/Statistics-Trends-and-Reports/ReportsTrustFunds/Downloads/TR2015.pdf.
9. Congressional Budget Office. The 2015 Long-Term Budget Outlook, June 2015.
10. Center for Medicare and Medicaid Center. NHE fact sheet, (an increase of Medicare, etc.). Available at: https://www.cms.gov/Research-Statistics-Data-and-Systems/Statistics-Trends-and-Reports/NationalHealthExpendData/NHE-Fact-Sheet.html.
11. The Facts on Medicare Spending and Financing, July 24, 2015 (expenses area). Available at: http://kff.org/medicare/fact-sheet/medicare-spending-and-financing-fact-sheet/.
12. Medicare spending by claims. (hospital expenditure and claims). Available at: https://www.medicare.gov/hospitalcompare/Data/spending-per-hospital-patient.html.
13. National Health Expenditures, Average Annual Percent Change, and Percent Distribution, by Type of Expenditure: United States, Selected Years 1960–2013. Centers for Medicare & Medicaid Services, Office of the Actuary, National Health Statistics Group, National Health Expenditures Tables (December 2014). Available at: https://www.cdc.gov/nchs/hus/contents2014.htm#103.
14. Gretchen Jacobson, Anthony Damico, Tricia Neuman and Marsha Gold. Medicare Advantage 2015 Spotlight: Enrollment Market Update. Kaiser Family Foundation, June 2015.
15. What is the Spending on Medicare? Available at: http://www.usgovernmentspending.com/us_federal_spending.php?view=6&chart=11-fed_12-fed_13-fed_14-fed&title=medicare_spending_analysis&meta=med.
16. Effect of Healthcare to spend on the US economy. Available at: http://aspe.hhs.gov/health/costgrowth.
17. Congressional Budget Office. *Medicare Baseline*, March 9, 2015.
18. Robert Farley. ACA impact on per capita cost of health care. *Health Affairs*, Posted February 14, 2014.
19. Source of information. Centers for Medicare & Medicaid Services (CMS). Available at: https://www.cms.gov/Research-Statistics-Data-and-Systems/Statistics-Trends-and-Reports/NationalHealthExpendData/NationalHealthAccountsHistorical.html.

20. Joint Point Regression Analysis. Available at: https://surveillance.cancer.gov/joinpoint/download.
21. Growth in Medicare spending by the beneficiary. (adjust expenses and beneficiary). Available at: https://aspe.hhs.gov/basic-report/growth-medicare-spending-beneficiary-continues-hit-historic-lows.
22. Medicare future budgets. Available at: https://www.cms.gov/Research-Statistics-Data-and-Systems/Statistics-Trends-and-Reports/NationalHealthExpendData/NHE-Fact-Sheet.html.
23. Keehan, S.P., G.A. Cuckler, A.M. Sisko, A.J. Madison, S.D. Smith, D.A. Stone, J.A. Poisal, C.J. Wolfe and J.M. Lizonitz. National health expenditure projections, 2014–24: Spending growth faster than recent trends. *Health Affairs* 34(8): 1407–1417, 2015. Available at: http://content.healthaffairs.org/content/early/2015/07/15/hlthaff.2015.0600.abstract.
24. The Trend in Medicaid Spending. Chapter 1. Available at: https://www.macpac.gov/wp-content/uploads/2016/06/Trends-in-Medicaid-Spending.pdf.
25. D. Bachrach, P. Boozang, A. Herring and D.G. Reyneri. 2016. *States Expanding Medicaid See Significant Budget Savings and Revenue Gains*. Princeton, NJ: State Health Reform Assistance Network and Robert Wood Johnson Foundation. Available at: http://statenetwork.org/wp-content/uploads/2016/03/State-Network-Manatt-States-Expanding-Medicaid-See-Significant-Budget-Savings-and-Revenue-Gains-March-2016.pdf.
26. Medicare Budget and Performance. Available at: https://www.cms.gov/About-CMS/Agency-Information/PerformanceBudget/index.html.
27. Mark V. Pauly. Should We be Worried about High Real Medical Spending Growth in the United States? *Health Affairs* [Web Exclusive], W3: 15–27, 2003.
28. Stephen Heffler, Sheila Smith, Sean Keehan, M. Kent Clemens, Mark Zezza and Christopher Truffer. Health Spending Projections through 2013. *Health Affairs* [Web Exclusive], 11 February, 2004.
29. L. Lorenzoni, A. Belloni and F. Sassi. Health Care Expenditure and Health Policy in the USA versus Other High-Spending OECD Countries. *The Lancet*, 384(9937): 83–92, 2014.
30. J. Holahan and S. McMorrow. Medicare and Medicaid Spending Trends and the Deficit Debates. *New England Journal of Medicine* 367: 393–395, 2012.
31. V. de Rugy. Facts on Medicare Spending and Finances. Available at: http://kff.org/medicare/fact-sheet/medicare-spending-and-financing-fact-sheet/.
32. T. Foertsch and J. Antos The Economic and Fiscal Effects of Financing Medicare's Unfunded Liabilities. October 11, 2005.
33. Safety Net Pool Care Program. Available at: http://federalsafetynet.com/safety-net-programs.html.
34. Health Care Safety Net Resources. Available at: http://federalsafetynet.com/safety-net-programs.html.
35. Medicaid Disproportionate Share Hospital (DSH) Payments. Available at: https://www.medicaid.gov/medicaid/financing-and-reimbursement/dsh/index.html.
36. Federal Medicaid Disproportionate Share Hospital (DSH) Payments. Available at: http://kff.org/medicaid/state-indicator/federal-dsh-allotments/?currentTimeframe=0&sortModel=%7B%22colId%22:%22Location%22,%22sort%22:%22asc%22%7D.

37. Disproportionate Share Hospital (DSH). The Medicare DSH Adjustment (42 CFR 412.106). Available at: https://www.cms.gov/Medicare/Medicare-Fee-for-Service-Payment/AcuteInpatientPPS/dsh.html.

38. Who is Paying for Medicaid? Available at: https://www.medicare.gov/your-medicare-costs/help-paying-costs/medicaid/medicaid.html.

39. How is Medicare funded? Available at: https://www.medicare.gov/about-us/how-medicare-is-funded/medicare-funding.html.

40. How does Medicaid Work? Available at: http://people.howstuffworks.com/how-Medicaid-works4.htm.

41. What are Medicare and Medicaid? *Medical News Today*. Available at: http://www.medicalnewstoday.com/info/medicare-medicaid.

Chapter 25

MACRA and the Merit Incentive Payment System

The Headache of MACRA

The Medicare Access and CHIP Reauthorization Act (MACRA) was created in 2015.

It permanently repealed the service related group (SRG) and eliminated the scheduled cut required, effective July 1, 2015.

This replaces the mingle for use in the value-based payment modifier battles and penalties, limited to 4%. This will be gradually increased to a maximum of 9% after 2021, based on a more specific target, and will lessen the use of patient resources to a greater extent than the current value-based payment modifier program, in which most of physicians and healthcare providers, including all accountable care organizations, long-term homes, hospices, etc. need to participate. This also comes with an incentive.

MACRA does many things, but most importantly it establishes new ways to pay physicians for caring for Medicare beneficiaries. The law also includes new funding for technical assistance to providers, and funding for the development and testing of metrics, and it enables new programs and requirements for data sharing and establishes new federal advisory groups. It is comprehensive legislation that has the potential to restructure US healthcare significantly.[1]

MACRA combines parts of the Physician Quality Reporting System (PQRS), Value-based Payment Modifier (VBM), and Medicare Electronic Health Record (EHR) incentive program into one single program called the Merit-based Incentive Payment System, or "MIPS."

CMS may not eliminate global surgical quotes—the value-based payment modifier intended to cover payment to physicians with high Medicare costs unless measure quality is equally high, and vice versa, caused the total cost per patient to not be limited to the fee-for-service that the physician performs.

The VBM does not adjust for risk—this is an issue in the demographic poverty status area with a cut for a physician who served the most disadvantaged patient population.

The new system pushed to report meaningful data, improve quality measurement, and try to limit the patient use of Medicare services by aggressive prevention.

MIPS considers actual performance improvement and risk to be based on cost quality and clinical practice improvement visits. This is supposed to be a better risk adjustment for a patient population, so a physician that takes care of people that are under-served will have less risk and fewer penalties.

The payments incentive penalty provision may be marginally better than the prior law for now and must be improved. The limits of the burden alone may drive more physicians to limit Medicare exposure. Medicare allows the physician to accept payment in full, but there is a mandatory claim to filing whereby, if the physician is not participating, he or she can choose to receive an assignment for Medicare but at a charge limited to 109.25% of allowable Medicare.

The patient receives a partial payment for Medicare. The physician is considered non-part when enrolled as a new provider of Medicare with a new tax ID number, unless he or she has sent in a partner agreement.

Some physicians will opt not to accept Medicare payments, except in an emergency. If there is a contract, the physician can cancel and opt out at the two-year anniversary with 30 days' notice.

MIPS AND QPP

The Centers for Medicare & Medicaid Services (CMS) require a physician to participate in the Quality Payment Program (QPP). There are two ways a physician can do this:

1. By MIPS
2. By advanced alternative payment methods (A-APMs)

Participation in MIPS is based on four components:

■ Quality
■ Cost
■ Advancing care information (ACI)
■ Improved activities (IA)

CMS expects to have at least six measures of quality reported, one of which must be an outcome measure. CMS will assign a point to the test according to their score. A measure that falls below the completeness threshold will receive 1 point. Small practices will gain 3 points for reporting a measure that does not meet the threshold. CMS has also suggested a qualified clinical data registry (QCDR) based on electronic medical record data (EMR), which will represent 50% of the final score.

Now MIPS has a cost. CMS calculates a baseline value of zero, which will change to 30% beginning in 2019. CMS will base the cost calculation on the total per-capita cost for all beneficiaries cared by a provider and their spending for that period.

Despite this, the ACI still needs to be reported to receive a score in 2018, with the support of an electronic health record, and the software needs to be updated almost every year, unfortunately. The ACI component represents 25% of the total score.

IA remains weighted at 15%; the physician must participate in documented IA activities for 90 days in a row. These are minimal points: 2 for rural area and 4 for city area.

Small Practices Are Out

More doctors will be excluded by CMS from participating in the MIPS in 2018. Physicians are excluded if they:

■ Are part of an A-APM
■ Have $90,000 or less in Medicare B billing
■ See 200 or fewer Medicare patients

This was a significant change from CMS requirements, under which the billing was increased from $30,000 to $90,000 and patients from 100 to 200.

These changes are expected to exclude 540,000 physicians who do not reach the required level. CMS, who changed this rule in November 2017, is intending to revisit the policy in the future.

Despite the rule, problems remain in this era of value-based services in healthcare. The quality and cost of patient care is not simple to achieve and can take years to learn.

Small practice (15 or fewer physicians) will still report their quality data earning bonuses in points from CMS under the MIPS program. They will be able to join the virtual plan for improving the ability to access rewards.

CMS is also getting into the performance category, which will account for 10% of MIPS. This is based on Medicare spending beneficiary and total per capita cost measures. This will not have required any acknowledgment from the provider since they are carried over the Value Modifier program.

What Is the Meaning of the Points?

While the aforementioned three points are the basis at present for participation in CMS reimbursement, this will increase to 15 points if the physician wishes to have an increase in his or her CMS payment by 2020; otherwise, he or she will receive penalties.

Comments on CMS Rules

In the navigation of these rules is quite tricky, and reading CMS reports can at times take days, since they are very convoluted. A physician that must see patients and do clinical work is hardly going to find the time to update himself or herself at all. Therefore, more physicians are joining practices, which requires higher overheads than solo training, and they will hire a manager, adding more costs to the rent. EMR and its update is another cost that practices must face.

Maybe the son of a friend of mine was right. His dad was a physician, but he chose to become a nurse and then a Certified Registered Nurse Anesthetist (CRNA), and he makes $250,000 dollars a year with no CMS or paperwork issues. Nowadays, physicians struggle to make the same money.

This is a situation that is not sustainable: CMS is spending lots of federal money, but punishing and restricting physician practice can be dangerous, and can drive physicians out of practice in the long term. Who is then going to take care of the patients?

Suggested Reading

1. What Is MACRA? NRHI. Available at: http://www.nrhi.org/work/what-is-macra/what-is-macra/.
2. What is MACRA and MIPS? Practice Fusion. 2016. Available at: https://www.practicefusion.com/blog/what-is-macra-and-mips/.
3. What's MACRA? CMS. Available at: https://www.cms.gov/Medicare/Quality-Initiatives-Patient-Assessment-Instruments/Value-Based-Programs/MACRA-MIPS-and-APMs/MACRA-MIPS-and-APMs.html.
4. MACRA: Disrupting the Health Care System at Every Level. Deloitte. Available at: https://www2.deloitte.com/us/en/pages/life-sciences-and-health-care/articles/macra.html.
5. The Medicare Access and CHIP Reauthorization Act (MACRA). National Partnership for Women and Families. Available at: http://www.nationalpartnership.org/issues/health/macra.html.

Chapter 26

Will Any Healthcare Ever Work? Single Payer?

A Million-Dollar Question

This is a million-dollar question. Indeed, we hope so, but the way that we are going, we are not sure if the federal CMS programs, Medicare and Medicaid, will remain or perish. Maybe private insurance will take over, but with skyrocketing costs placed on the consumer. To start to understand where we are going, let us go back a little and restart from the origin of Medicare and Medicaid.

In the U.S. private insurance market, patients purchase coverage; different people end up with different insurers, and there are multiple payers throughout the healthcare system.

In a single-payer system, there is just one payer—typically the government. The government provides coverage, and no private insurers are involved.

Many governments instead pay for *most* but not *all* of their citizens' medical treatment. In these countries, people have the option to buy "supplementary" private insurance, which pays for services, such as dental care, that the government healthcare program excludes. People often also have the choice to buy "complementary" private insurance, which covers the copays and deductibles in the government's insurance plan.[1]

Insurance Dilemma

U.S. government entities spend more per capita on healthcare than all but two other countries in the world. The two advanced economies with the most economically

171

free healthcare systems—Switzerland and Singapore—have achieved universal health insurance while spending a fraction of what the U.S. spends.[2]

According to the *NY Times*, "Given the enormous size of our private for-profit health insurance sector, and the overwhelming influence of money in our political system, the chances that insurance companies could be forced into nonprofit status are incredibly remote. This leaves us with some single-payer as the only viable option if we are to achieve a real universal coverage."[3]

Regardless of any cost-benefit comparisons of universal healthcare coverage plans in developed countries, the writers are playing down the most critical issue: Every other developed country offers some coverage for all of its citizens. We do not. This is immoral and should be the line-in-the-sand feature of any health care plan under discussion.[4]

It is less complicated to find physicians who take Medicare than employer-based healthcare insurance. The overhead and medical care costs are supposed to be much lower under Medicare than under private insurance.[3]

Medicaid: Possible Approach

Medicaid in 1965, under President Lyndon Johnson, came as a drastic expansion of the safety net established by Social Security in 1940. It was created to cover the catastrophic medical bills of people without insurance. It was afterwards expanded to children and disabled people also. Today, one out of five Americans, or about 70 million people, use Medicaid. This is creating more pressure in the federal government, given the fact that Medicare is crashing and Medicaid is collapsing, and they don't have enough funding to cover the whole population. Many people are proposing different solutions such as time limits on Medicaid benefit copayment, but no solution likely to make a difference has yet been found. Some states such as Maine have proposed to make Medicaid share with the physician. For instance, the beneficiary would be required to make a premium payment before starting college. Imposing a $20 copayment for improper emergency room use will enable the physician to charge the beneficiary for a missed appointment. As a physician, I agree with this proposal. The patient takes advantage of his or her status, and doesn't show up at the office for an appointment for the day of surgery. Patients use the emergency room as their doctors and providers because they don't have to pay. There is no repercussion for abusing the system. Therefore, some limitation is required. States like Arizona have been implementing the Medicare 1115 waiver to create a program that only covers acute care. Flexibility is vital in the design of new Medicaid programs because the state owns the funding for the program. After the act was passed, the number of Medicaid users grew. Previously, some adults could not receive Medicaid cover unless they were making less than $12,000 a year. Medicaid is now being expanded to cover adults without children who are making less than $16,000 a year.

It seems that every state in general and the federal government will increase the number of people covered by Medicaid, and therefore the funding available in each state will be out of balance. Overuse of the emergency room or doctor's visits by Medicaid users need to have some impact. The physician needs to be part of this by documenting when a patient comes to the emergency room simply to receive, for example, their antibiotic medication or next pain pills. Taking Medicaid away from people who are not working is not a solution because some of these people have a good reason for being unemployed.

In general, Medicaid and Medicare are insurance systems, like the social system in other countries, but regulated by the federal government and controlled by the state. Being administered by the federal government but controlled by the state creates a different silo. Federal law needs to create a balance between the application of Medicaid in the United States and among the different states.

Single Payer

Rick Ungar[5] reported in *Forbes* that

> there is ample reason to believe that the conversion to a single-payer system will go some distance in solving some cost issues. Right now, the for-profit model sucks about $400 billion a year out of our health care dollars to pay for administrative costs—costs that mostly disappear in a public system where administrative costs run dramatically lower. That's a lot of money that could be better spent on providing actual care to those in need.
>
> The notion of creating a "Medicare For All" health care system in America has been on the table ever since Medicare first came into being in 1965. And for just as many years, the battle has raged over whether making such a system available to all Americans would be akin to a capitulation to socialism in a nation that prides itself on its free-market principles or, conversely, an easy and moral step forward for our society.

Ungar also wrote:

> However, if the for-profit insurance companies find it no longer worth their while to stay in business, which is the feeling to be shared by Mr. Bertolli of Aetna, a single-payer system may be the only solution for our politicians when government is the only entity large enough to take on the financial responsibility of our health care system.
>
> Whichever side draws your support, if the war over the Affordable Care Act has taught us anything it is that there is likely to be more

than enough legislators to block an effort to extend Medicare to all Americans, or some other variation of a single-payer system, for the foreseeable future. Given we the lack of independence given by the corporation one single payer is even closer than ever.

In the *Harvard Business Review*, Dr. Sandro Galea[6] wrote in July 2017 about the single-payer situation in the U.S.:

> Some critical players remain opposed to a single-payer system. One is the American Medical Association. It favors an ACA-like structure that subsidizes insurance for low-income individuals and families and argues that a single-payer system would stymie private-sector innovation, create long waiting periods, and offer less patient choice. However, the AMA is far from a disinterested party. Indeed, it was an early resister of alternatives to our current fee-for-service system, fearing a more progressive model could diminish the independence and entrepreneurial capacity of its members.

Not surprisingly, insurance and pharmaceutical industries, which have a strong economic self-interest in maintaining the status quo, are also against the single-payer model. Opponents warn that a single-payer model could lead to a wholesale bureaucratization of the healthcare system by the federal government, or even to socialized medicine.

Again, Galea mentioned:

> Canada has had a single-payer model for decades, and there's no government takeover of its health care system in sight. Most services are still provided by the private sector, and most physicians are still self-employed. While health expenditures remain high, Canadians nevertheless enjoy better health outcomes at lower cost than the United States, whose population's health is mediocre despite ever-higher spending on medical care. In this system, the doctors maintain their independence.
>
> While such innovative payment models are possible within the current fragmented payer systems, a single-payer system immediately creates an opportunity for wide-scale adoption of new approaches that can transform health in the United States. With a health system reoriented toward stopping the disease before it starts, rather than treating it once it strikes, we may even begin to see more health investments go beyond health care, targeting the social, economic, and environmental factors that create the conditions for disease in society.

The current system is still pay-as-you-go, without any focus on prevention or on strengthening the physician and healthcare system to avoid excessive expenses in the emergency room and hospitals, which is one of the financial nightmares for the current system.

Notes

1. Kim Soffen. 2017, October 17. Single-Payer Would Drastically Change Health Care in America. Here's How it Works. *The Washington Post*. Available at: https://www.washingtonpost.com/graphics/2017/national/single-payer-explainer/?noredirect=on&utm_term=.b6f3905e38ab.
2. Petition Congress: Universal Health Care. Change.org. Available at: https://www.change.org/p/congress-universal-health-care.
3. Can a 'Single Payer' Health System Work in America? 2017, September 19. *The New York Times*. Available at: https://www.nytimes.com/2017/09/19/opinion/health-care-single-payer.html.
4. Lanhee J. Chen and Micah Weinberg. 2017, September 19. The Sanders Single-Payer Plan Is No Miracle Cure. *The New York Times*. Available at: https://www.nytimes.com/2017/09/19/opinion/sanders-health-care-medicare.html.
5. Rick Ungar. 2012, February 23. Single-Payer Health Care Is Coming To America-Are We Ready? *Forbes*. Available at: https://www.forbes.com/sites/rickungar/2012/02/23/single-payer-health-care-is-coming-to-america-are-we-ready/#2fca33071857.
6. Sandro Galea. 2017, July 18. Is the U.S. Ready for a Single-payer Health Care System? *Harvard Business Review*. Available at: https://hbr.org/2017/07/is-the-u-s-ready-for-a-single-payer-health-care-system.

TOWARD THE PERFECT SYSTEM – WHAT NEEDS TO BE DONE AND WHERE WE NEED TO GO

VI

Chapter 27

Patient Engagement, Education, and Prevention Started on the Local Level

Healthcare Starts with Patient Self-Care

The only way that we can start solving the puzzle of healthcare in the United States is by patients taking more responsibility for their health. This means that they need to actively look for the best way to live their life healthily.

Most patients do not take care of themselves and come to see a physician thinking that he or she has a magic wand to fix them, but by then it is too late.

The general population tends to justify this behavior. But this is not excusable anymore.

How is it that a high-school student can build a company, making millions of dollars, but cannot learn how to take care of his or her health?

God gives us health, and we had better keep it in order as we have only one life.

On top of this, I have seen patients in Asia, Europe, and South America, from less developed societies, who were taking care of themselves by following simple cultural and traditional practices and family practices.

These people are eating fruit and vegetables, walking every day, and taking herbs for digestive problems or headache without calling the doctor.

My mother, who is 80, lives in Italy and goes to the gym three times a week, walks for 1 hour every day, and eats a healthy diet, not an exuberant one like we are used to in the U.S. She takes tea to aid digestion and a glycerin suppository if needed, without the use of medications. She is therefore not obese, and she does not visit the doctor unless she needs to.

These simple principles can be found in excellent healthcare systems like those in Norway, Sweden, or Germany, where the healthcare system works and takes care of the patient very well. In Asia, homeopathic medicine is used where possible. I follow my grandmother's advice and rarely take medication for headache, pain, sleep, or gastritis. I bought myself some herbal tea the last time I went to Mexico and still use it with success. This is to show that is all a state of mind and good or bad habits.

The psychological need to see a doctor is often more important than the prescription received. It gives peace of mind. I have experienced that a patient can become upset with me because I did not prescribe anything to him or her. The patient did not need anything, but the act of coming out from my office with a prescription can make patients feel better as they have achieved something, or confirmed that they are actually sick.

If you do not prescribe anything, the patient may go to another doctor and speak negatively about you, saying that you do not understand his or her pain and problems. This practice creates a society with extreme needs for no reason, and this can only get worse.

Prevention

An old saying points out that the best medicine is prevention. Coming from a social system country, I understand prevention quite well. Under the social system, it is essential to see a primary care physician. You have to wait and wait for an appointment. You cannot just show up. If you need emergency care, there is a physician at the local level that provides that service. If you want a mammogram, you have to wait 6–9 months, meaning that you have to think about it and start scheduling it a year in advance before you turn 40 years of age. Patients therefore have direct involvement in and responsibility for their care, which is lacking entirely in the U.S.

Patients in social system countries try in general not to see their primary care physician and instead to try different things including herbal treatments and homeopathic medicine. They also try to follow the basic rules for a good life—exercise, no smoking, and limited alcohol consumption—because they know that it is difficult to see a doctor. People living to an older age follow these suggestions and fully support preventive medicine. When they are sick, they don't go to the emergency room—they go to the primary physician covering emergencies in their region. Emergency room overuse is a significant problem in the U.S.

If you have a cold, you cannot go to the emergency room as you will be rejected or placed on a waiting list for 8–24 hours. Emergency rooms need to treat emergencies. Therefore, other issues can wait. You will not die from a cold.

Pharmacy and medication costs are regulated by a certain amount of out-of-pocket expenses, which are very low, but at the same time can affect people of lower economic status. Therefore, patients tend not to buy extra medicine if they don't need to. Pharmacies are typically not open 24 hours but usually close at 7 pm, after which you have to find one that is open late. It sounds counterintuitive, but in making the patient more responsible, he or she tends to use the pharmacy less and to judge the need to go to the doctor or the pharmacy. This decreases overuse of the system.

These systems decrease also the continues call to top the doctor to get or refill the prescription, so the physician can see the patients and not get interrupted by the social call and not for clinical necessity.

The social system is also regulated by a certain amount of medication that the patient can get. Shopping for doctors is not the solution to get treated. Buying for opioids is not possible, which avoid crises as we have in the USA.

Patients Abusing the System

A physician friend of mine told me a story about a mother who called at 2.30 in the morning because her child was crying because he was teething. He did not start that night. The mother of a child is supposed to be ready for this healthy stage of development. We all went through it, and most of the time we asked our mothers or grandmothers what to do. In this situation, what a physician can do is likely the same thing that a grandmother can do. That type of phone call creates animosity between patient and physician. The physician gets stressed out and cannot take care of more critical issues, and the family is dissatisfied with the physician's response because they think that the physician has a magic pill for teething pain.

Just because you can call a physician 24 hours a day doesn't mean that you should. Another example was a patient yelling down the phone at 2 o'clock in the morning because she could not go to the bathroom. This had been going on for a week. What did the patient do? Nothing—she continued to eat as normal. Instead, she should have stopped eating, taken more water, hot tea, or soup, and maybe a glycerin suppository and more fiber. There is not much you can do at 2 am. She was not happy. Therefore, she went to the emergency room. Since we live in an antagonistic society, the emergency room doctor ended up doing a full laboratory test, chest X-ray, electrocardiogram, and a CT of the abdomen to make the diagnosis that she was constipated.

How much does this cost society? Is it better to reserve CT scanning for trauma patients or those with a real clinical disease? This is a case where the patient needs to be penalized and fined. Constipation is a chronic problem, and if the patient does not take care of it, nobody can.

Maybe, even in this case, the expertise of a mother or grandmother could have been used to take care of the problem at 2 am. I think that a fine and penalty would make the patient think twice before calling the physician.

The problem is that some of patients want everything ready for them.

The system is broken because the culture is broken. And to change the culture of the patient means that we will never have a good system because most patients overcall their physicians and engulf the emergency room, creating a hefty weight on the healthcare system that will cause it to crash.

Another friend of mine was called at 1 am by a mother asking the physician to order a pregnancy test kit at the pharmacy because she believed her daughter might be pregnant.

First of all, pregnancy kits are available over the counter, but the mother wanted a prescription since she was on Medicaid, and Medicaid will discount the price. Second, she should have been ashamed to call somebody to take care of a situation that can happen in life. Instead, all she cared about was abusing the system and getting Medicaid to pay for it.

Penalties for Abusive Care

There needs to be some monetary fine for patients who come to the emergency room without a real reason.

I suggest a points system, like for driving licenses; when you reach 6 points, you must pay a fine.

Another way that the overuse of the emergency room can be resolved is to place more physicians in a region with urgent care access so that the physicians can see patients with urgent problems in their office.

The problem for the physician is that patients can speak badly about their physician online. Web pages that grade physicians never check on the patient's story and the physician gets stuck with a negative review that has nothing to do with his or her ability. This system affects healthcare tremendously. The issue is that nobody is defending physicians from unreasonable patients. It seems the physician is always wrong and the stupidity of the patient is never brought to light.

The same thing is valid for lawsuits. The U.S. is a "lawsuit happy" country—we all know this. But in healthcare, we need to put a stop to it. It is ok for a patient and a lawyer to sue. But let's adopt some of the rules of European countries: if the judge or the court finds the suit to be frivolous, the suing party needs to pay the expenses of the trial and the lawyer.

This will cut down on frivolous suits. There is no repercussion on the patient for bringing frivolous lawsuits, but there are repercussions on the physician if they do not do their job correctly. This is not right.

We expect the physician to fix everything or to be able to touch patients and cure them. Health issues need to be prevented first and taken care of medically when they are a problem.

In the past, the grandmother's solution was applied in all circumstances, but now we are forgetting the basics of how we can take care of our health on our own.

We have lost that touch because it is much easier to blame someone else or the physician.

Healthcare Starts at the Local Level

It seems that, in the U.S., every health issue is an emergency or a tragedy. The lack of primary physicians on a local level that can help the patient is perhaps as important as the culture and the knowledge of the patient. We need more physicians at the local level. These physicians need to be supported financially by the city and county. They will not be able to support their own family by seeing patients without insurance or those that refuse to pay $30 in copayment but walk into the physician's office with a new Louis Vuitton bag, new iPhone 10, and expensive shoes.

If they are not supported, most physicians will not see these patients and will instead send them to the emergency room.

Politicians need to understand that healthcare starts at the local level, with the involvement of city and county funding. Physicians do home visits and urgent care, like in Europe. The primary physician base needs to be enlarged before they can even think about reforming the healthcare system.

Healthcare reform in the U.S. needs to start in the rural areas and the cities, and not from Washington.

Suggested Reading

1. Marcella Nunez-Smith, Elizabeth H. Bradley, Jeph Herrin, Calie Santana, Leslie A. Curry, Sharon-Lise T. Normand and Harlan M. Krumholz. Quality of Care in the US Territories. *Archives of Internal Medicine* 171(17): 1528–1540, 2011. Available at: doi:10.1001/archinternmed.2011.284.
2. The Changes that Could Improve Health Care in Our Country. *The Virginia Daily New.* Available at: http://www.virginislandsdailynews.com/opinion/the-changes-that-could-improve-available-health-care-in-our/article_54da9664-5551-506e-a2d0-8d349189939c.html.
3. Sara Allin and David Rudoler. The Canadian Health Care System. *The Commonwealth Fund.* Available at: http://www.commonwealthfund.org/topics/international-health-policy/countries/canada.
4. Quality Improvement Organizations. *The American Health Quality Association.* Available at: http://www.ahqa.org/quality-improvement-organizations.
5. T. Kue Young and Susan Chatwood. Health Care in the North: What Canada can Learn From its Circumpolar Neighbors. *CMAJ*, 183(2): 209–214, 2011. Available at: https://pdfs.semanticscholar.org/2ea1/db166371ef81b1118a9b07074bb5dcd1a9b8.pdf.

Chapter 28

Population Health Initiatives: Teen Obesity Crisis

High-Cost Insurance

Because of the high cost of insurance in the U.S. healthcare system, people are going to the emergency room for their care, and this increases the cost of healthcare and overruns the emergency room, taking space from the people that need it.

When I see a patient without insurance or Medicaid, I am afraid that most of the time that person has not taken care of him or herself and ends up discovering all of his or her problems upon admission to the hospital for a simple hernia repair.

This is not allowed in social systems where everybody needs to take care of themselves as best as they can.

Population Health Initiatives

The challenge for physicians is to improve the overall well-being of a population which is now diverse and complex.

Some of the challenges, for example, are: (1) newly diagnosed cancer patients in rural communities; (2) expecting mothers who smoke and have no obstetric physician; (3) retired Asian or African American female patients with multiple physicians and prescriptions at various pharmacies in several cities; (4) Hispanic migrant workers without benefits suffering work-related injuries; (5) the mental health of post-war veterans without appropriate support; (6) the treatment of chronic disease; (7) opioid control and crises; (8) and the disparity between populations and health, among others.

Unfortunately, the list is getting longer every day, and our healthcare system must find a way to take care of everybody.

In this chapter, we focus on one of the biggest problems in the U.S: obesity in teenagers.

A Change in Thinking

In the U.S., the obesity crisis is reaching the highest level in the word. There must be a reason for this. Patients do not understand what obesity is, and therefore it is very difficult to treat them. A 200-pound adult is not at an average weight; a 50-pound 8-year-old is not normal. Despite this, it's challenging to tell patients that they have to lose weight, and it is very difficult with an obese child to convince the mother (who is also usually obese) that her child is overweight!

Sedentary lifestyles have also been affecting weight in the U.S., along with smoking, alcohol.

High-School Teaching

This sort of lifestyle is not healthy. To take away these things would be impossible. The only possible solution is to educate people, starting from high school, because that's the only time that you can have the full attention of the future adult population.

Obesity Crisis

I recently published an article in the *Journal of Obesity and Nutritional Disorders*[1] about obesity in young people, and the next section is taken mostly from that article.

Thirty-five percent of adults in the U.S. are obese, and about 32% of children and adolescents in high school are obese. Nearly half of all American adults have one or more preventable diet-related chronic diseases, including cardiovascular disease, type 2 diabetes, and overweight and obesity (2015–2020 dietary guidelines). Our goal is to achieve good health and wellness, though it is important to know the difference between the two; health[2] is the "state of being free from illness or injury" while wellness[3] is the "progress toward achieving good health and maintenance."

But why is this important? Students in high school are one step away from becoming adults and taking on responsibilities, one of which is taking care of their health. There are three things to consider before beginning the journey toward a healthier lifestyle, including a change in diet; thus a diet plan, and an exercise plan might help.

Schools need to make sure that students are getting health check-ups from their doctors. It is up to the school to provide students with healthier meals that are going to benefit them nutritionally. With the help of the school in ensuring healthy diets and providing enjoyable physical activities, every student will have the opportunity to have a healthier life and to prevent themselves from becoming obese.

Approaching a change in diet, an exercise plan, and fighting obesity can seem challenging, but it is possible.

To Help the Help Initiative

The HELP philosophy provides a basis for making healthy lifestyle changes possible. The acronym, HELP, characterizes an essential part of the ethos: **Health** is available to **Everyone** for a **Lifetime,** and it is **Personal**. Physical activity is not just for athletes, it is for everybody. It is essential to adopt and sustain healthy habits early in life to increase long-term health, wellness, and fitness. Everyone must take personal responsibility for learning and using these skills. Health is more than freedom from illness, disease, and debilitating conditions. Students need to take into consideration that every single one of them is unique. Each person's characteristics influence their health and wellness. We all have personal limitations and strengths. Some dimensions that involve health-related physical fitness are body composition, muscular endurance, strength, power, cardiorespiratory endurance, and flexibility. Having robust cardiorespiratory endurance will allow the heart, blood vessels, blood, and respiratory system to supply nutrients and oxygen to the muscles and give them the ability to utilize fuel to allow sustained exercise.

Diet

The importance of proper nutrition for optimal health is well established. Most people believe that nutrition is important but still find it difficult to maintain a healthy diet. The first step is to change the food that is served in the cafeteria, in order to change students' diet. For students to achieve a healthy lifestyle, eating healthy plays an important role. Eighty percent of weight-loss is diet, and only 20% is exercise. Therefore, nutrition outweighs training when it comes to an overall change in the body. Schools need to address the average calories that high-school students should be consuming every day.

Designing a Diet

A high-school boy between the ages of 14 and 18 should be consuming anywhere between 2,200 and 3,200 calories a day.

A high-school girl between the ages of 14 and 18 they should be consuming anywhere from 1,800 to 2,400 calories. It is therefore important that schools ensure appropriate meals for both males and females.

In Table 28.1, activities and calories are matched and reported, showing the number of calories indicated according to age and activity level.

This table is important and should be reviewed before suggesting any diet to a student.

A 1,800-calorie diet is advisable for students who do not exercise.

Exercise

Having good physical fitness will allow anyone to have energy at the end of the day, even if they have worked productively. Regular physical activity can increase life span. Living longer is essential, but being able to function efficiently during all the years of life is equally, if not more, important. Many benefits of health, wellness, and fitness are obtained from moderate amounts of activity, so the key is to be at

Table 28.1 A Chart to Help in Estimating Caloric Intake in Young Adults

| | Activity Level | | | | | |
| | Male | | | Female | | |
Age	Sedentary	Moderately Active	Active	Sedentary	Moderately Active	Active
14	2,000	2,400	2,800	1,800	2,000	2,400
15	2,200	2,600	3,000	1,800	2,000	2,400
16	2,400	2,800	3,200	1,800	2,000	2,400
17	2,400	2,800	3,200	1,800	2,000	2,400
18	2,400	2,800	3,200	1,800	2,000	2,400
19	2,600	2,800	3,000	2,000	2,200	2,400

least active enough to receive these benefits. All people benefit from physical activity, but the benefits are unique for each person. Heredity, age, gender, ethnicity, lifestyle, current fitness level, health status, and a variety of other factors make each person unique at any point in time. The principle of individuality indicates that the benefits of physical activity vary from individual to individual based on each person's unique characteristics.

For high-school students, it is essential to understand the five basic types of physical activity. Each step represents a step toward achieving health, wellness, and fitness. Any physical activity can be combined with another, but each will have its unique benefits.

Cardiorespiratory endurance is probably the most important aspect of physical fitness because it has a significant impact on health and dramatically influences physical performance. A person with good cardiorespiratory endurance can persist in physical activity for relatively long periods without undue stress. The heart, blood vessels, blood, and respiratory system need to supply nutrients and oxygen to the muscles. Once oxygen is delivered, the muscle tissues must be able to use oxygen to sustain physical performance. It is important to note that the beneficial effects of cardiorespiratory endurance on risk for heart disease and early death are independent of these other effects.

Exercise is an integral part of students' lives and provides them the health benefits they need. Exercising helps prevent obesity, increases endurance, reduces the risk for certain diseases, and delivers nutrients to the body's muscles and tissues. Exercise should be balanced and should include both cardio and weight lifting to get the most benefit.

Conclusion

Building a healthy lifestyle can be challenging, but worthwhile. Finding inner motivation will make a difference. It can help to write down a plan and set short and long-term goals, with self-monitoring to accomplish goals. Individuals who make a change will be able to live a long, healthy, and fit life. Fitness can promote a robust immune system and influence susceptibility to illness.

Notes

1. Eldo Frezza, Mariah Dutchover, Shyla Ervin, Joshua Watson, Jordan Hendricks, et al. Fighting Obesity: The Benefit of Diet and Exercise for High School Students. https://gavinpublishers.com/articles/Editorial/Journal-of-Obesity-and-Nutritional-Disorders/Fighting-Obesity-The-Benefit-of-Diet-and-Exercise-for-High-School-Students.
2. Wellness. *Merriam-Webster*, n.d. Web. 26 July 2017.
3. Health. *Merriam-Webster*, n.d. Web. 26 July 2017.

Suggested Reading

1. Executive Summary. 2015-2020 Dietary Guidelines for Americans, N.p., n.d. Web. 26 July 2017.
2. Changing Your Habits for Better Health. National Institute of Diabetes and Digestive and Kidney Diseases and U.S. Department of Health and Human Services, 01 May 2017. Web. 26 July 2017.
3. Getting Your Vitamins and Minerals from the Diet. *Harvard Health*, N.p., n.d. Web. 26 July 2017.
4. Estimated Calorie Needs per Day by Age, Gender, and Physical Activity Level. *CNPP USDA*, N.p., n.d. Web. 26 July 2017. Available at: https://www.cnpp.usda.gov/sites/default/files/usda_food_patterns/EstimatedCalorieNeedsPerDayTable.pdf.
5. About NIH Obesity Research (Obesity Research). National Institutes of Health and U.S. Department of Health and Human Services, n.d. Web. 26 July 2017.
6. Research for Your Health. National Heart Lung and Blood Institute and U.S. Department of Health and Human Services, 23 February 2017. Web. 26 July 2017.
7. Before You Start an Exercise Program. ACE Fit | Fitness Information. N.p., n.d. Web. 26 July 2017.

Chapter 29

Clinician Involvement in Improvement Initiatives

Physicians' Complex Relationships

Physicians' relationships with the many different facets of the healthcare industry can be complicated and can present a wide variety of ethical and moral considerations. As the U.S. medical system struggles to control costs, determine appropriate care, and allocate resources, many new challenges face the healthcare system. Physicians' relationships with that system are essential, for as we have witnessed on multiple occasions in the past two decades, when physicians are not intimately involved in the design and structure of changes in the system, the resultant modifications may be contradictory to good medical practice. This could continue to alter the most important of all relationships in healthcare, the physician-patient relationship.

Expectations Based on Quality

There is a lot of hope regarding quality, particularly now that the healthcare system is changing—everybody looks at quality as a savior for the future. But quality has always been there throughout different generations.

The healthcare system is struggling with the recruitment and retention of physicians. Burnout has had an emotional cost for hospital managers in the healthcare system.

Finger-pointing toward different departments is common. Firing emails from firms or hospitals from the administrator are unlikely to make any progress toward organizational goals. Physicians must find a solution whereby they can save the healthcare system from people who are trying to manipulate it as well from people that are in healthcare for financial reasons and not for the care of patients.

The goal of any strategic plan focuses on financial success and growth and usually includes nothing about the quality of services offered to the patient. A large part of the strategy is to sell the hospital as "a great place to work." But it is not necessarily "an easy place to work."

Organizations set and establish plans and strategy focusing on margins and never on the quality of care and quality of life of providers such as physicians and nurses, who most of the time have to work in a hostile environment and therefore are unable to provide the best standard of quality and care.

It would be good to also talk about having a higher focus on quality providers in healthcare, and not just a focus on margins. Some organizations focus on what to extract from a community while the physician spends time in the community helping patient. By assisting the patient in serving the community and ensuring good quality, the financial margin is going to be good.

Physician Recognition and Appreciation

Discussions about physician appreciation and recognition are complicated. Like most people, physicians like to be appreciated for their personal and professional contributions. At the same time, many physicians feel that "the Golden Age" of medicine is the past and that they are in fact underappreciated by a society that accords celebrity status and outlandish wealth to athletes, actors, and "pop icons." Physicians are reeling from an overhauled healthcare system that is run for the most part by nonphysicians and continues to devalue physician efforts while rewarding the CEOs of large healthcare corporations with ever-increasing compensation packages. Reimbursement for medical care, the "deliverable" of our health system, is considered an "expense" that interferes with the profits of the insurance industry. The major satisfaction of physician appreciation, the response of a grateful patient, has been eroded in a system that interposes the "payer" between the doctor and the patient. In these times, one may indeed wonder how the physician is recognized for his or her contributions and whether in fact there is appreciation for the considerable effort physicians exert to attain and maintain a level of professional excellence. To discuss the issue of recognition and gratitude, we need to first consider the forces that influence physician satisfaction.

One of the great attractions of the medical profession is that it offers an infinite array of environments in which to work, each with different challenges and rewards. One may choose a simple clinical practice or basic research, academic, private, or institutional method or combinations of the above.

Central to physician satisfaction is a sense that he or she is appreciated, recognized, and respected for his or her achievements, past and present. For the practicing physician, acknowledgment by a grateful patient, student, or respected colleague are the most common everyday measures of satisfaction. Sometimes, no external support is necessary; merely one's own recognition that a problematic diagnostic riddle was solved or a critical experiment was completed is sufficient. For the academic physician, peer recognition by publication and promotion play a crucial role. Those engaged in research can add intense competition for funding to this list. The critical element in all these scenarios is that the contribution made by the physician to the "other" (whether it is the patient, student, or scientific community as a whole) is overtly acknowledged. While an aspect of this appreciation may involve monetary compensation, financial compensation without recognition is insufficient. Most prizes awarded to physicians, whether for service or scientific discovery, are valued much more for the award itself than for any monetary value. Similarly, promotion and tenure continue to be valued in academic medical centers, despite the increasing dissociation between tenure and monetary compensation in many cases. This is consistent with prior comments made on the importance of reputation and recognition rather than material compensation. Some physicians derive indirect recognition from their relationship with a "first-quality" institution, whether academic or clinical. This recognition by association is rarely enough in itself to satisfy most physicians unless acknowledgment and advancement accompany it within the institution itself.

Physician Sensitivity

Physicians are very sensitive to being treated respectfully. While the physician of today can no longer expect to be "put on a pedestal" or afford to have a "god complex," many physicians bridle at being "one of the team" and indistinguishable from "licensed independent practitioners" or administrators. One may argue the point, but most physicians expect that their level of training and the degree of responsibility they have for life-and-death decisions should set them apart from other members of the "healthcare team."

While they do not wish to be considered infallible, most expect that their opinion is given more weight than that of other members of the "healthcare team." Group recognition is essential, but not in itself sufficient for most physicians. Ensuring the recognition of individual physician contributions in a meaningful way is critical. This should occur within the day-to-day environment in which the physician works.

Value, Real Value

The value of healthcare in the hospital is not just something that you can write on a website, but physicians need to lead and show the way. All personnel need to buy into the culture, from housekeeping to medical staff and from nursing to administration executives. Consistency in the cultural spread throughout the system is what will allow this generation and the next to accomplish the primary mission of keeping healthcare alive and focused on its real meaning, which is taking care of the health of people.

Corporations have expanded around the country, buying hospital after hospital with the purpose of margins and making profits while forgetting about patients. New hospitals are hiring physicians and nurses just for the staff, but the quality is not checked.

Most of the time, the people who hire physicians and nurses don't understand healthcare as they never were busy physicians or nurses themselves and therefore never understand the difference between a good nurse or an excellent physician and a lousy nurse or lousy physician.

Healthcare is also measured by the effort and the soul that these people put into their work compared with those who come to work just to get the hours done. Healthcare is something that you don't just do for the sake of it. You do it because you believe that it is a mission, not just a job.

The corporation should have the same belief, but sometimes the corporation buys a hospital to make money, or to lose money as a tax break. Such a hospital is always going to be of low quality, although the local community does not know that. I have seen this first-hand. Of course, the corporation will deny it, but most of the staff can see it but cannot talk otherwise they will pay through repercussions or a sham peer review.

But their silence is not helping to build a better healthcare system for the future. Busy physicians should be promoted earlier and not at the end of their careers.

Physician–Administration Relationship

The responsibility of a physician is to practice evidence-based medicine to a high-quality standard. We need to involve and invest patients in their care decisions. We need to be available all the time. We need to establish working collaborations with other physicians. Education and research are going to always be part of the medical profession, even in non-academic practice.

Physicians must also learn how to treat people with respect, but they also need to be addressed with respect themselves. Physicians need to take leadership and ownership of the quality of service and even the financial aspects of patient hospital and clinic flow and patient billing.

On the other side, hospital administration needs to perform strongly in recruiting and retaining physicians by sharing with the physicians a culture that is good for the administration, for the hospital, and for the patient. Corporations also need to learn how to treat physicians—too many times, we have witnessed that physicians are treated without respect.

Just as physicians need to be respectful to staff and patients, corporation administration needs to be respectful to physicians and nurses, not just with words but with facts!

Communication, including all business decisions and strategic plans, needs to be shared with physicians. We expect clarity on goals and how physicians are evaluated. Physicians that like to learn should be supported by giving them more time and opportunities for continuous medical education as well as more funding.

Physicians should be evaluated not just by the number of patients treated but also by the quality of their work and the relationship they have with other healthcare providers. Rumors do not count! Gossip does not count!

Healthcare organizations need to embrace the transition of physicians from clinical to administrative work because, at the end of the day, physicians study to become what they are because they believe in patient care and healthcare. Most of the administration end up in healthcare by changing jobs, not because of belief in or passion for healthcare.

Therefore, physicians are always going to have quality and the patients in mind, and if they understand the business, the goals, the culture, and the finance, then they can be outstanding administrators and can make healthcare better.

Suggested Reading

1. E.E. Frezza. *Principles of Ethics for Surgeons*. Chapter 8.
2. K. Wentlandt, N. Degendorfer, C. Clarke, H. Panet, J. Worthington, R.F. McLean and C.K. Chan. The Physician Quality Improvement Initiative: Engaging Physicians in Quality Improvement, Patient Safety, Accountability and Their Provision of High-Quality Patient Care. *Healthcare Quarterly* 18(4): 36–41, 2016.
3. Bryan Oshiro. 6 Proven Strategies for Engaging Physicians—and 4 Ways to Fail. *HealthCatalyst*. Available at: https://www.healthcatalyst.com/proven-physician-engagement-strategies.
4. Ilene MacDonald. 2017, December 15. IHI 2017: Strategies to Engage Physicians in Leading Quality Improvement Initiatives. *FierceHealthcare*. Available at: https://www.fiercehealthcare.com/healthcare/ihi-17-strategies-to-engage-physicians-leading-quality-improvement.
5. Committing to Physician Quality Improvement. *ABMS*. Available at: http://www.abms.org/initiatives/committing-to-physician-quality-improvement/.
6. B.M. Wong, C.M. Cheung, H. Dharamshi et al. Getting the Message: a Quality Improvement Initiative to Reduce Pages Sent to the Wrong Physician. *BMJ Qual Saf*, 21: 855–862, 2012. Available at: https://psnet.ahrq.gov/resources/resource/23478/getting-the-message-a-quality-improvement-initiative-to-reduce-pages-sent-to-the-wrong-physician.
7. Michael T. Rapp. CMS 2009 Incentive Programs. *CMS*. Available at: https://www.cms.gov/Medicare/Quality-Initiatives-Patient-Assessment-Instruments/PQRS/Downloads/PQRI_Implementation_4_MR.pdf.

Chapter 30

Physician Involvement in Management and Team Building

Leadership

It is important for physicians nowadays to learn teamwork and learn how to be a leader. Defining successful leadership can be a challenge. "Leader" is a generic term for anyone who takes on a role of authority or provides direction in particular circumstances. For instance, surgeons are leaders in the operating room, orchestrating teams of skilled professionals through complicated procedures, charged with ensuring the best outcome for their patients. Many become leaders in their chosen specialty, developing better, more efficient methods of operating, fine-tuning skills, and training others to follow suit.

Leaders can also be seen as those who organize "labor" into efficient units and monitor the distribution and use of capital assets and its progress. The leaders continue to monitor and evaluate progress, making adjustments along the way to ensure that development is maintained and efficiency is increased wherever possible.

The role of a leader is as varied as the types of leadership styles employed by individuals. Leadership style has less to do with success than does the individual. Successful leaders command respect, instill inspiration and vision, appreciate the thoughts and ideas of others, and cultivate an environment of growth and continuous improvement.

Types of Leadership Style

Leadership styles can be summarized into three categories:

1. Autocratic: The autocratic leader makes decisions without reference to anyone else. There is a high degree of dependency on the leader; this approach can create de-motivation and alienation of staff. It may be considered valuable in some types of business where decisions need to be made quickly and decisively.[1]

2. Democratic: Democracy encourages decision-making from a variety of perspectives, utilizing a process of consultation before decisions are taken. In this environment, leadership may be emphasized throughout an organization. The persuasive leader makes decisions and seeks to persuade others that the decision is correct. The democratic style may help to motivate and involve others, fostering a feeling of ownership in the firm, development of ideas, etc. While it improves the sharing of ideas and experiences within the business, it can delay decision-making. Democracy is congruous to any company that relies on creativity and good interpersonal relations and excellent teamwork.

3. Paternalistic: The paternal leader acts as a "father figure" while making the decisions. However, unlike the autocratic leader, the protective leader may consult with others and believes in the need to support staff.

Decision-Making after Analysis: The SWOT Framework

All leaders need to make decisions, and therefore they need to be familiar with the SWOT structure (Table 30.1).

Communication between Healthcare Teams

Effective communication is characterized by the shared purposes of intent and collaboration. Team members value familiarity over formality. Healthcare team members need to trust each other and ensure cooperation toward a common goal, that of providing the best care possible for their patients.

Table 30.1 SWOT Structure

Internal		External	
Strengths	Weaknesses	Opportunities	Threats
Positives		**Negatives**	
• Strengths • Assets • Resources • Opportunities • Prospects		• Weaknesses • Limitations • Restrictions • Threats • Challenges	

This is difficult in a time of increased demands on healthcare providers, staff, and teams, when there seems to be a gap or disconnect between the members of healthcare groups. To get there, we need to identify our roles, leadership, accountability, and proper staffing and ensure that the right training is available to define the roles and responsibilities of each member of the team. I believe that checks and double checks, accountable members, adequate supervision, and supervisor training should be in place. Equipment should be available and should be in line with what is available in comparable institutions. The team needs to learn how to use this equipment. We should not just use "fillers" to do a job—we need to be trained personnel because, above all, it is healthcare, and outstanding healthcare, that we all strive for. Huddles, code training, and code of conduct should be implemented on a regular basis. The moral of the team needs to be addressed, as well as their frustrations and concerns. Respect for team leaders needs to be emphasized.

The physician leader should assess the situation and make a recommendation using techniques such as:

SBAR: Situation Background Assessment Recommendation

A team leader should be identified, and team spirit should be built. Roles for each member and understanding the role and limitation. Skill training should be available. Essential equipment should be available to the hospitals, teams, and physicians. Safety and monitoring outcomes should be implemented.

The assessment and previous discussion of issues related to tasks should be evaluated using the following technique:

STICC: Situation, Task, Intent, Concern, Calibrate

This is a structured briefing protocol, used by firefighters. It is based on five steps:

1. Situation: Here is what I think we face
2. Task: Here is what I think we should do
3. Intent: Here is why
4. Concern: Here is what we should keep our eye on
5. Calibrate: Talk to me. Tell me if you don't understand, can't do, or know something I do not.

CMO Role

A chief medical officer (CMO) is typically the physician in charge at most hospitals. The person in this position must have a medical degree and can practice in the medical field but should also have experience in managing others.[2]

The primary responsibilities of this position include overseeing all doctors and making sure that patients are safe and well cared for. A CMO does not usually have to provide direct medical care to patients.[3]

But a useful CMO should also be an experienced physician who has been working in the trenches. This way, physicians will look to him or her for suggestions and not disregard him or her as ignorant.

I have worked with many CMOs, and for some of them I am trying to figure out if they ever went to medical school!

The CMO role is considered a leadership position since doctors look to this person for guidance, so previous leadership experience is helpful. Additionally, communication and interpersonal skills are often needed since the CMO should be able to relate to doctors in all fields and needs to talk frequently to department managers, patients, and top executives.

One of the significant tasks of the CMO is to ensure that doctors are delivering the best care possible for patients. This means that this person typically trains new doctors on hospital policies, evaluates the level of care given by medical professionals, and chooses medical directors. The CMO also deals with finances, as he or she typically determines the rate of pay for employees, assists in funding, and helps manage the budget.

The nonphysician-CEO likes to see three essential behaviors in the CMO: a reflection of profoundly transformational qualities, e.g. a passion for quality and safety; encouragement of teamwork and collaboration; and a commitment to the mission and values of the organization.

It is extremely important that CMOs possess good problem-solving skills, as this is likely a profoundly transformational quality. It typically takes the form of a collaborative act rather than a solo exercise. But this has to be based on substantial clinical experience and the capability of understanding the different specialties and exposure to the daily routine of the hospital.

"Your physician colleagues will believe you have gone to the dark side and your administrative associates will consider you an enigma," according to an article by David Longnecker.[4] He continues: "Although this may be hyperbole, it emphasizes the unique role of the CMO as an intermediary between the organizational components of the organization and the clinicians who teach, investigate, and practice in that organization. Because of their experiences as both physicians and administrators, CMOs may offer insights into the unintended consequences of policy and administrative decisions that may not be apparent to those who have not had both experiences."

Most important perhaps, is that the business model imposes its hierarchy, which is neither physician nor patient-centered. While it may seem that CEOs of many corporations are imperial or even despotic, their underlying obligation is to better the organization. Failure to do so is virtually the only grounds for dismissal.

A fundamental commitment to the organization, rather than to the individual or to central principles, is foreign to the culture of most physicians. The tension between physicians and healthcare organizations is further increased by the fact that physicians are not highly valued (at least in their role as physicians) in many of these organizations.

Physicians as Leaders

Physicians, by nature, are adaptable. Medicine is not an exact science, and too often things don't go as planned. These same characteristics make a physician a good leader. Whether in private practice, hospital administration, academics, or within the community, flexibility will always be a valued and appreciated attribute. Of course, the degree of adaptability required is relevant to the situation. Within the hospital environment, the reputation and culture of the institution may dictate one particular leadership style, such as autocratic or democratic. The method may also change the environment based on particular circumstances. As in the case of the hospital example above, one situation may call for a leader to use a more autocratic approach to decision-making and yet another to use a democratic method.

This requires transformation such as changes to a business or organization, as well as long-term strategic planning, clear vision, and goals that are applicable to the industry and not to a general idea. Quality physicians as leaders and as possible CEOs of hospitals are the future goal.

How to Be a Leader

There are several concepts that can be initiated that will go a long way toward enhancing leadership. Any plan for improvement begins with a subjective assessment of how well an individual is currently performing in a leadership role. Consideration should be given to the tone and objective of messages that are sent, either written or verbal. The focus should be on reducing negative messages that are sent out through everyday actions and interactions, externally and, more critically, internally.

A regular review of internal processes is recommended to reduce or eliminate problems. Whether it is for a business, surgery training program, hospital, or any other organization, periodically taking stock of how well specific programs or procedures operate provides vital clues to their effectiveness, as well as other relevant factors such as employee, customer or patient satisfaction, and economic growth. When a leader exhibits efforts to understand system flaws and organizational inefficiencies, he or she demonstrates to others (employees, patients, staff, etc.) that the leader identifies with the organization. His or her credibility is thus enhanced.[5]

Successful Leaders Focus on the Positive

During self-evaluation their success, leaders should ask themselves: What did my staff do well today? In response, the goal should be to try to:

1. View negative issues in a positive light. In other words, there's always an opportunity for learning and improvement.
2. Reiterate this by complimenting the employee(s) for raising awareness of the issue so that it may be addressed.
3. Identify a process whereby the leader and employee(s) can work better together for greater success.
4. Continue to coach the performance and standard of care by ensuring that everyone understands the goals and expectations, and if they do not, to find out what can be done to help.

Input is critical to identifying the issues surrounding hospital personnel, patients, and physicians. In the case of a physician, it can be the quality of life in the practice and satisfaction of the physician. With staff, it may be the input/output issues where difficulties arise during the day and need to be resolved. The goal of a good leader is to create a thriving team environment because, while the playmaker is an essential part of the team, he or she will not win the game by his or herself.[6]

Treat Colleagues as Customers

Providing feedback, both positive and negative, is essential in any good working relationship, but most importantly in the role of leader/subordinate. Feedback should be provided either in writing or with an appreciation table so that the subordinate understands whether the input is in a compliment zone or a critical area. The information must also include a plan for creating goals with the assistant where everyone wins, and it should be communicated that achieving success requires the contribution of the aide. Make sure the physicians know everyone wins in the process.

Sometimes a Leader but Always a Physician

The best leaders know that some issues require their focused attention above all else. In the case of physicians, the emphasis should be on their patients. Physicians should take the initiative to periodically view the practice from the patients' perspective. What is the patient experience? Are the patients treated with respect? Is their time valued? Are their health issues and concerns being addressed? One of the most critical strategies in the office is to warm up the environment. The patient should feel comfortable, not anxious.

It is also imperative for physicians to understand the dynamics of communication, and to be aware of how they are communicating and what message the patient is receiving.[7]

Often, the problems between physicians and patients arise through a misunderstanding, both verbal and non-verbal. Communication between the surgeon and the patient is give-and-take. The best way for physicians to ensure that they are being understood is to ask questions that address issues such as whether the patient's pain is controlled and whether his or her concerns have been adequately addressed.[7]

The physician should always have the patient's best interests in mind, and make sure that the patient knows that he or she is going to be treated accordingly. The simple acronym TEKE can be used to remember the patient approach: "T," introduce yourself and talk to the patient; "E," explain how the evaluation and diagnostic workup will be performed; "K," keep the patient informed; and "E," explain the conventional method of care and treatment to the patient.

T	Talk
E	Evaluation
K	Keep informed
E	Explain treatment

Notes

1. Andrew Jameton and Jessica Pierce. Environment and Health: 8. Sustainable Health Care and Emerging Ethical Responsibilities. *CMAJ*, 164(3): 365–369, 2001.
2. Organizational Structures in a Medical Center. *Salubris*. Available at: https://sites.google.com/site/salubrisocilha/organizational-structures-in-a-medical-center.
3. Job Profile: Chief Medical Officer. *Top Master's In Healthcare Administration*. Available at: https://www.topmastersinhealthcare.com/job-profiles/chief-medical-officer/.
4. David E. Longnecker. *Public Policy & Aging Report*, 24(3): 126–127, 2014.
5. David E. Longnecker, M. Patton, and R.M. Dickler. Roles and Responsibilities of Chief Medical Officers in Member Organizations of the Association of American Medical Colleges. *Acad Med*, 82(3): 258–263, 2007.
6. P.J. Norwood. 2015, October 21. Positive Leadership Traits. *Fire Engineering*. Available at: https://www.fireengineering.com/articles/2015/10/positive-leadership-traits.html.
7. Jack G. Zosky. 2004, March 1. Immediate Implant and Immediate Temporary Acrylic Crown in the Aesthetic Zone: A Case Report. *OralHealth*. Available at: https://www.oralhealthgroup.com/features/immediate-implant-and-immediate-temporary-acrylic-crown-in-the-aesthetic-zone-a-case-report/.

Chapter 31

The Perfect System

Utopia

Sir Thomas More (1477–1535) used the Greek word *eu-topos*, meaning "a good place," to define a perfect society in an imaginary world called Utopia. Utopia was a complex, self-contained community living on an island where all the people shared life and ideology, culture, and life cycles. He raised the question of the possibility of living in a perfect world and society. His goal was to envision this ideal society in response to the chaos of European politics during his lifetime. It was a platform to define the errors and mistakes of the present community by visualizing the perfect world. Of course, his hopes and ideology were not matched, and the word *utopia* became synonymous with something that will never exist and can apply to society, ideology, politics, and way of life. The results of this application have only one outcome: will never happen.

Are we facing the same problems with healthcare? Are we trying to fix and remix healthcare following a utopist idea of a better world that exists only in our imaginations?

Transforming Healthcare

Apparently so, since we are close to imploding the healthcare system in the United States in a significant crash which will resemble the stock market crash in the 1930s. Lots of talk and lots of political and economic interests are at stake, and all the players want to gain something.

The issue is that they want to gain something through speculating on the health of American citizens. This is not a business; therefore all the reforms are failing. We have been treating healthcare as a business, but it is not a factory, people do not care or cloths; each one is different, and the difficulty is that you never know where they are going. It is like watching a live game—you never know who is going to score until they score.

Attempts have been made to apply a lean process from factories to healthcare. The problem is that the people who are trying to do this are factory ex-employees and therefore have no knowledge of healthcare. Therefore, a physician with experience of business will be better suited to lead the system. Without political attachment or favoritism, though!

Let's Apply Lean Business Concepts to Healthcare

The goal of healthcare is quality, which is complicated because it relates not to the color of a car, or how the seats move up and down, but to a human being who reacts in a certain way to a particular treatment. The goal is to make treatment as standardized as possible and to focus on adapting the process to each patient by following procedures, decrease deviations, and being ready to adjust to situations, just as a defense player in football will adapt to different schemes that the opposite team quarterback will call.

Quality focused: The goal of all healthcare is quality, quality of the care that physicians and nurses give to patients, but also quality of life for nurses and physician, as happy staff lead to happy patients and you want the team to enjoy coming to work as they will treat the patients better. Culture and situations where the hospital is supportive and not seen as a punisher or jail zone should be created. The application of standard operating systems, algorithms, etc. is imperative. These need to be implemented by capable physicians and nurses for their peers and not by business people interested in the bottom line and unaware of the complexity of healthcare. Everybody needs to do the job they are trained to do. The use of physicians with administration capabilities is therefore highly recommended.

It has been shown that hospitals with stable CMOs have perfected their quality metrics and relationships with physicians and have subsequently improved their finances.

Sometimes you need someone to watch and understand the process before going deep into it without knowing what needs to be fixed.

Bad quality: This will impact financial stability as it can incur penalties and extra costs such as extended hospital stays and the use of resources that will affect the bottom line of the hospital.

Yogi Berra, the New York Yankees catcher, has said that "you can observe a lot just by watching." This sentence is as true as in healthcare nowadays. Too many times, we try to fix a process without understanding what is wrong with it.

Toyota Lessons

The Toyota car manufacturer is a leader in lean processes and has used this to streamline production. Let's first review what their concept is and then apply it to the healthcare field.

Sensei is the Japanese word for teacher. Many teachers needed to implement a system that works, so it is better to have a teacher who is specialized in what he or she preaches for peer-to-peer teaching.

Muda means futility, uselessness, or wastefulness.

Jidoka refers to automation with a human touch. This is a control measure for better quality. It is based on four principles: (1) identify an anomaly, (2) stop the process to fix the anomaly, (3) fix the process and get back on track, and (4) determine the cause of the initial problem. This can be applied in healthcare to identify the cause of an issue, which is done during risk management as cause analysis of a sentinel event.

Heijunka means smoothing the production process, achieving a standardized work process. In healthcare, this means how to approach, process, and care for a patient, which we can also achieve using protocols or algorithms for clinical quality.

Andon is a system to notify management, maintenance, and other workers of a quality or process problem. The centerpiece is a device incorporating signaling lights to indicate which workstation has the problem.

Poka-joke means mistake proofing. Watch the system to find the error and check it so that you can fix it together with the people that made the mistake so that now you have a team decision and approach.

Kaizen (kai = people; Zen = better) is a change for the better and respect for people (need to treat people with genuine respect). Who are the customers? Patients and physicians. It is also a constant search for better delivery and relationships.

Kanban is an inventory system for replacing used products. In addition to low costs, it also focuses on having the inventory replenished at all times for quick delivery to the manufacturing area. A good product is better than a cheap one, since it will be used once and forever.

What Needs to be Done: Perfect Throughput

The system and the hospital need to focus on these lessons as follows:

Jidoka: set protocols with a human touch
Heijunka: establish protocols or algorithms for clinical quality
Andon: implement a system for the notification of quality or process problems
Poka-joke: realize any mistakes in the process

Kaizen: (kai = people; Zen = better) constantly search for better delivery and relationships

Kanban: replenish the inventory for better delivery

By following the above concepts, the hospital can achieve a reasonable throughput, which is the goal of any system.

Hospital Throughput: This is the process followed by the patient from when he or she arrives at the hospital outpatient department or the emergency room through his or her care and discharge. This is important, because a standard and smooth output will enable the hospital to take care of many patients by making sure that everything is done in a timely and high-quality manner so that the patient can go home, also in a timely manner. It is imperative to remove all obstacles from this process to avoid creating bottlenecks that will affect all the departments of the hospital. This is similar to when having a plug in the pipe—all the water comes back up and start to spill over.

Facilities Need To Be User-Friendly and Respectful

User-friendly facilities: Patients want to know where the emergency room, the bathroom, or the registration office are, so the hospital needs to be set up in a way that is clear and user-friendly for patients and staff to navigate: Supply room accessible, operating room moving like a well-oiled machine, etc.

Respect for people: This also means respect for the patient's family, as well as for doctors and nurses. These are the components of the working team—yes, the patients and the family should be included in this group and have to work together for better results. Nurses and physicians need to work well with their peers, and the hospital needs to build a friendly and cohesive culture.

Avoid Lone Star Situations or Compartmentalized Hospitals

Avoid system–hospital silos: The only way a hospital or a system will be successful is if each department and area works together. Creating a silo in one area will decrease productivity and obstruct throughput, which will take time to fix and reset.

The Hospital and the Physician Need to Understand the Process

Value Stream Map (VSM) is a good approach in manufacturing but not in healthcare and should be replaced by Process Map (PM) because, in healthcare, you provide a service that is different for different patients—it is not just building the same car and changing the color.

Process Map (PM) involves utilizing strategies to identify bottlenecks, classify process steps, and evaluate value-added and non-value-added processes. In healthcare, one step at a time must be considered since you cannot fix the entire process like building.

Standard Work in Process (SWIP) is the minimum component, in our case patients, to ensure a stable flow. It is also the minimum inventory that will provide patient care. This is reached by balancing the process and eliminating full waste steps, combining operations, and adjusting staff numbers. As a value-added process, these are things that are better for the patients, while business value-added items include the need for care to be delivered without impacting on the responsibility.

First Change the Culture, Then Change the System

First change the culture, then change the system; by doing the opposite, people will feel imposed upon and the attempt will fail. People fail in their normal behavior or follow the path of least resistance, so changing their culture will help to make them project and infuse in them a new reason for reaching goals and performing.

The most crucial element, again, is to ensure a cultural transformation, and only people can create this—improvements and changes need to be applied by leaders.

We need not choose what the most straightforward path is, but what the right track is. How do we decide which one is right or wrong? The right track is the one that gives the best quality of care to our patients. This is the goal of healthcare: if the quality is there, the finances will follow.

Care, therefore, should be organized around the patient and not around the healthcare system.

A status board with suggestions from staff should be implemented and the suggestions should be followed; otherwise, you will lose the team.

A committee where physicians can be outspoken without being punished for telling the truth should also be implemented.

A system without complaints is a dream; the problems are there and is the duty of the system to fix them.

Work should be standardized to obtain improvements as with the lean philosophy used in manufacturing. However, healthcare is not manufacturing, therefore it should be possible to change the path toward the best care when needed.

Nowadays, with the use of electronic medical records, there is no more room for fragmented care—the goal is to achieve quality care across specialties and the healthcare organization, creating patient profiles that can be easily accessed in encrypted models. That will also decrease the abuse of medication, specifically of opioids, since the patient would not be able to shop around for meds across different hospitals.

This system of care and integration needs to be implemented in its entirety by physician leaders and nursing leaders, who are the only ones that can assure quality-delivered care. Therefore, physicians need to work with healthcare organizations on the front line, not on the side or as a limited part of it.

Suggested Reading

1. Utopia. Wikipedia. Available at: http://history-world.org/Utopia_T.pdf.
2. Lean Manufacturing. Wikipedia. Available at: https://en.wikipedia.org/wiki/Lean_manufacturing.
3. The Lean Approach for Improving Performance and Optimizing Added Value: Concepts and Benefits. *Manavue.* Available at: http://www.manavue.ca/si_mve_a/Lean_Approach.html.
4. Robert B. Pojasek. Lean, Six Sigma, and the Systems Approach: Management Initiatives for Process Improvement. *Environmental Quality Management,* 13(2), 2003. Available at: https://pdfs.semanticscholar.org/dfc4/d74406e15ed-1afe39da8eb1299bf101c5a4b.pdf.
5. Asif Mahmood and Francesca Montagna. Making Lean Smart by Using System-of-Systems' Approach. *IEEE Systems Journal,* 7(4): 536–548, 2013.

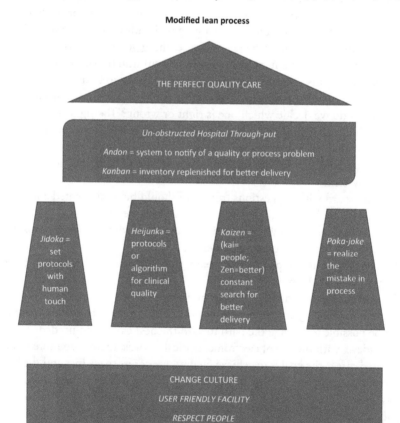

Modified lean process

THE PERFECT QUALITY CARE

Un-obstructed Hospital Through-put

Andon = system to notify of a quality or process problem

Kanban = inventory replenished for better delivery

Jidoka = set protocols with human touch

Heijunka = protocols or algorithm for clinical quality

Kaizen = (kai= people; Zen=better) constant search for better delivery

Poka-joke = realize the mistake in process

CHANGE CULTURE

USER FRIENDLY FACILITY

RESPECT PEOPLE

CHANGE SYSTEM APPROACH

THE PERFECT SYSTEM

Index